Resurrection
Love-Life

Barbara Dent

PAULIST PRESS
New York/Mahwah

The publisher gratefully acknowledges use of the following material: excerpts from *Autobiography of a Saint,* translated by Ronald Knox, courtesy of Franciscan Press of Quincy College; excerpts from *The Complete Works of St. Teresa of Avila* and *The Complete Works of John of the Cross,* both translated and edited by E. Allison Peers, courtesy of Gordon-Press Publishers; and verses from *The Jerusalem Bible* by Alexander Jones, ed., copyright © 1966 by Darton, Longman & Todd, Ltd. and Doubleday, a division of Bantam Doubleday Dell Publishing Group, Inc., used by permission of Doubleday, a division of Bantam Doubleday Dell Publishing Group, Inc.

Library of Congress Cataloging-in-Publication Data

Dent, Barbara.
   Resurrection love-life / Barbara Dent.
     p. cm.
   Includes bibliographical references.
   ISBN 0-8091-3405-5 (pbk.)
   1. Spiritual life—Catholic authors. 2. Faith. I. Title.
BX2350.2.D448   1993
248.4'82—dc20   93-11006
                                                    CIP

Published by Paulist Press
997 Macarthur Blvd., Mahwah, N.J. 07430

Printed and bound in the
United States of America

Contents

DEDICATION

For Kathleen Chave
my lifelong, intimate friend
and sister of the heart,
who died August 23, 1989

"Au revoir, darling, not goodbye."

Author's Note

In this present book I continue where I left off in my previous one, *My Only Friend Is Darkness.* That book's last chapter was entitled, *Risen in the Lord: Emergence and Freedom.* Now *Resurrection Love-Life,* as its title indicates, examines in detail the inner spiritual state, and its outward manifestations, of those who have emerged from entombment with Jesus to share his risen life's "glorious liberty" and the love it pours forth for the world.

This resurrection love-life induces various forms of prayer which I also describe.

Some of the terms I have coined to fit my themes are as follows:

The first syndrome: Sin / Suffering / Evil. This represents the unredeemed state in human beings from which have developed the horrors, past and present, of our life on this planet, including our desecration of our physical environment. Jesus became incarnate in order to render this syndrome null and void. He invites us to continue his work through his extended incarnation and continuous passion which are operative in and through us till the end of time.

The second syndrome: Love / Suffering / Prayer. Through this second syndrome the Spirit enables us to transmute the negative energies of the first into positive, creative powers for blessedness both personal and collective. In this syndrome we live in conscious union with Jesus and involvement in his healing and saving act and the spiritual transformation it brings.

The third syndrome: Love / Joy / Fulfillment. This third syndrome celebrates the victory of grace through our cooperation with it and the fulfillment of the divine indwelling. It is the equivalent of what has been called transforming union and spiritual marriage. It is an essential element of resurrection love-life, which is unimpeded spiritual union with the risen, glorified Lord who transmits his liberation to us and through us to others.

Whoever remains in me, with me in him, bears fruit in plenty, for cut off from me you can do nothing.

—Jn 15:5

Remain in my love . . . so that my own joy may be in you and your joy be complete.

—Jn 15:11

As you sent me into the world, I have sent them into the world. . . . Father, may they be one in us, as you are in me and I am in you. . . . I have given them the glory you gave to me . . . have made your name known to them and will continue to make it known, so that the love with which you loved me may be in them, and so that I may be in them.

—Jn 17:18; 21, 22, 26

We know that by turning everything to their good God cooperates with all those who love him, with all those he has called according to his purpose. They are the ones he chose specially long ago and intended to become true images of his Son, so that his Son might be the eldest of many brothers. He called those he intended for this; those he called he justified, and with those he justified he shared his glory.

—Rom 8:28–30

The Pool
of Tranquillity

I shall tell you a story.

There was once an old woman, somewhat infirm in body and
muddled in her mind, who lived alone in a little log cabin in a clear-
ing in the woods. It was not a deep forest, but a beech wood on the
lee side and lowest slopes of the mountains against which the pre-
vailing, rain-bearing winds beat.

In this wood were many open, sunny glades, and it was in one
of these that the cabin was. It had been built many years before by
an early explorer in the area, but since then some facilities had been
added, and its simplicity and the peace of the surroundings suited
the old woman's needs perfectly.

She sat often on a wooden seat just outside her door where
the sun came through the treetops and made a pool of warmth and
light. She would cup her hands upward in her lap, rest her head
against the house wall, lift her face to the sun, close her eyes, and
gently ease herself into the timeless moment.

Sometimes she would play her flute to the birds, who, inquisi-
tive and unafraid, came down on lower branches to peer at her, or
gathered near her feet on the ground to hop about and peck at the
soil for insects, worms and the crumbs she would throw there for
them.

She tended her little garden in its sunny spot, cooked her simple meals, conversed with her dog (who, she was sure, understood
every word), wrote poems and allegories, and went for long walks

with Dog through the woods, up the hill slopes, and on good days even as far as the snowline.

Every fortnight her grandson rode in from the farm on the river flat below to bring the supplies she needed. She kept a few fowls and a rooster in an enclosure under the trees, letting them out each day to scratch and feed in the rich humus and among the bushes. Their droppings made good manure for her garden. She was a practical and resourceful old woman who used what was at hand for her simple needs.

It was a life that had hardships, but these were no handicaps when measured against the peace of solitude—which the birds, fowls and Dog did not disturb—and silence—except for the sounds of nature, and the constant sense of enfoldment in tender hands that cupped her as carefully as she did a butterfly, or newly-hatched chick, or Dog's faithful head resting on her knee in trusting love.

Happiness was too limited a word for the blessedness that saturated her. It was a serene, wordless, quiet bliss that filled her to the brim, like . . .

Like the water that welled up so mysteriously in the pool enclosed by a rocky outcrop in an open space surrounded by ferns not far from the cabin.

Although she had good rainwater in her tanks, she went twice a day to the pool to drink and to bring back a big bucket of its pure, crystalline contents.

She called it The Pool of Tranquillity. And sometimes The Pool of Siloam, for she knew she herself had been "sent" by the Master, like the blind man in her Good Book, to live here, and though she didn't bathe in the pool for fear of sullying its waters, she did drink from it. And the water she took to the cabin she used to cook with, to water her garden and to bathe any part of her body that needed healing. And there was no denying that her health was good for her age. The vegetables from her garden that were her staple food, and that she cooked in the water, always tasted delicious, and the garden itself flourished. Also any graze or cut or ache that her body experienced healed quickly after being bathed.

There was a legend that, aeons before, the Master of Love and Life had come into these woods to bless the creatures and the trees, and, finding the cavity in the rock and pitying its emptiness, blessed it too. Straightway the waters began to fill the space, bubbling up through clefts at its base, and not ceasing till the pool was brimming.

It was said that the Master then immersed himself in it, and from that time the waters had a special quality that made them sacred.

The old woman often thought about this ancient story, and sometimes she wrote poems on its themes, and sometimes as she drank from the pool, her heart cried out, "Maranatha!"

Mostly the water in the pool was so still that she could easily discern in its pure depths the secret that was its mystery and wonder. On the sandy bottom diamonds and crystals lay carelessly in little clusters or singly. Others rested, half concealed, in tiny crevices and hollows in the pitted rock. They were the treasure of the depths that only certain kinds of eyes could see, and every time she gazed at them in awe, she felt the presence of the Master and she worshiped him.

Glinting softly on this treasure, the light revealed pale lusters of color that delighted her, and it made different facets shine like tiny suns as it moved with the passage of the sun overhead.

Minute, darting fish, silvery like the diamonds, paused and palpitated, then were off again in a shimmer of graceful movement. At times they moved in shoals as if they were a single thought in a single mind; at others they rested, one here, one there, still as tiny pebbles.

In places delicate, green water weeds grew from the sand, motionless when there was no current to make them sway. Their lacy fronds rested in the water while the shoals of fish darted among them like children playing hide and seek.

The pool was fed from some hidden artesian spring. At intervals she saw it making the sand stir and lift while almost invisible bubbles rose to the surface, and stray eddies moved the water weed and made the fish swoop upward in glee.

"It is the artesian upwelling," she decided, "that is the source of the diamonds," for after each inflow there were always a few more of them lodged haphazardly here and there, reflecting the light, still, pure, everlasting, radiating some mysterious vitality of their own.

She had no desire to dredge them up from the depths. She did not want to own them, but was content to be certain they were real and not an optical illusion, and to experience the blessing that passed into her through them.

Tranquillity, undisturbed by the almost imperceptible flux from the hidden spring, was the usual state of the pool when she leaned over it to contemplate its beauty and scoop up its waters in her hands to drink deeply. Always she respected it as a wonder of the Master's manifold creation given to the whole world, and only temporarily in her care, since it was she who had discovered it soon after she first came to live in the unfrequented woods.

However, there were times when the waters became an agitated swirl, so that she herself was afflicted with disquiet because of it.

Two opposing kinds of disturbances intermittently produced the commotion.

One was when the gentle easing in of the artesian waters turned into a mighty upsurge from some hidden source pressing for release from the rock strata. Then all was turbulence. The tiny fish darted into refuges in the deeper rock clefts. Some of the delicate fronds of the water weeds were torn off and tossed to the surface. Granules of sand were forced up by the fierce currents and whirlpools so they too surfaced.

And there, also swirling, were diamonds and crystals, borne up by the ferment and held floating by its upward thrust. She could have grabbed handfuls but forbore to touch, ready to weep over their secret beauty so helplessly torn from those still depths.

The other kind of turmoil was just as elemental though dramatically different, having a threatening, evil aspect and power to terrify.

This invasion happened on nights so dark that only creatures with night sight could find their way through it. She herself dared not venture outside the cabin, but listened, taut, from within its solid walls, trembling while the hair on her neck and head stirred atavistically.

Some nameless, cumbersome monster came shambling toward the pool, crashing through the undergrowth, growling and grunting to itself as it went. Soon other noises suggested it had plunged huge, unwieldy paws into the waters—perhaps its whole furred, stinking body—and was splashing and lunging about till the once tranquil pool sounded like rapids roaring and rushing in a mountain canyon.

She was disturbed not so much by the danger to herself and Dog of some possibly predatory beast, as by the thought that the pool was being desecrated and fouled. She lay in frozen stillness, ears strained as the creature's tumult was answered by that of a rising wind moaning in the treetops, and by the clashing of boughs. Her eyes searched the night outside her window, trying to glimpse the monster and comprehend its nature, but clouds hid moon and stars, and the invader remained only a darker darkness in the night's obscurity.

Sometimes it played—if its activities could be called play—for hours, sometimes for only a few menacing minutes. Then, with a last defiant roar, it would crash its way back into the depths of the forest to what she supposed was its subterranean lair.

"I'll leave here first thing in the morning," she would resolve. "I can't stay while things like that go on happening. I can't bear the Master's pool to be violated."

Yet, when daybreak at last came and she went in dread to view the desecration, inconceivably everything was as it had always been. No sign of damage or pollution. The diamonds glimmered in the serene depths, the fish darted, the water weeds held up their fronds like palms of tiny hands in prayer, and the surface of the pool was so calm she could kneel there and contemplate each detail, wondering, her own hands clasped in thanksgiving.

Even the undergrowth round about seemed undisturbed. There was not a single sign of the creature's midnight depredations.

Had she imagined it? Dreamed it? Been under a delusion?

No—it had happened. She was certain.

The horror still afflicting her was real, not a form of self-deception. She remembered everything too vividly and her relief at deliverance was too immense.

It had been no nightmare—except in the sense of a living one.

She did not leave her hermitage because of the beast's visitations nor for any other reason, but stayed on year after year, until her white hair was sparse, her hands gnarled and trembling, her body bent, her gait slow, and Dog almost blind and ready to die during his prolonged slumbers.

She would stroke his head as he lay by her feet where she sat in the sun outside her door, her face lifted as ever to the sky, and he would feebly thump his tail in response.

Each day she went slowly and painfully to the pool, but only once a day now, and she carried back less water, for her strength had failed. More importantly, she had less need to drink it, for it was as if she herself had become just such a pool—lucid and quiet to her depths, safe from desecration by any wild beast, incapable of closing off herself from the constant, gentle invasion of those limpid waters that welled up uninterruptedly from deep in her own heart.

And now, seeing her age and infirmities, her grandson urged her to leave her cabin to live with him and his family on his farm on the plains, where his wife would look after her, but she courteously refused while she thanked him once again for his years of faithful service.

"I belong here," she told him, her eyes on the track that led to the pool. "The Master brought me here, and when it's time for him to take me away, he'll come himself to fetch me. There's no need to be alarmed about anything at all. Everything is as it should be. All is well, and I am ready to go in peace with him whenever he appears."

She stroked his brown, well-muscled arm. "You have been a good grandson to me, and I bless you. I leave the pool and all in it to you and your family. Guard it faithfully from the beast of the night, and speak of it only to the Master's pledged servants. He will guide you, after he has taken me with him."

When next the young man came, he found the fowls and their chicks loose in the glade, and the old woman peacefully in the sleep of death on her bed in the cabin. Dog was stretched cold and still on the floor beside her. Clasped against her shrunken breast was a small glass vial full of water and what looked to him to be diamonds.

She was smiling.

Later, on the far side of the glade, he came across a huge, ape-like creature, curled up just as peacefully in apparent sleep, but on careful examination it too proved to be dead.

We all have within us a pool like the one in my little story. It is what makes us human beings, for it is our entry permit into eternal life, infused into us when we are conceived. Its dimensions, capacity, shape, vary from one person to another. We are born with it and we die with it, but it does not die when our body does.

Some never become aware that it is within them—though the tendency to need and seek it does seem universal. Such spiritual defectives, though they may excel in other aspects of human living, miss out on the one essential for multi-dimensional existence.

Some, though they know the teaching about it, disregard the pool's existence, affirming only worldly values. They have but a small, overgrown pool, and it seldom if ever is stirred by the inflowing waters. It becomes stagnant if indifference is coupled with an evil life. Then it swarms with all kinds of nasty little creatures, and the ape-like brute takes possession of it, fouling it constantly. Finally it becomes so polluted that it dies.

Many who have some notion that their pool is there rarely visit it, being too involved in distractions of varying intensity, though they are not sinful. Year after year they procrastinate about checking their pool's condition—whether the waters are alive with the silvery fish and the delicate water weeds; if any diamonds are in it; whether the brute is desecrating it; the degree of impurity; the density of overgrown plants, weeds and straggly bushes that have established themselves all around it, almost hiding it; above all, its relevance to their own lives so cluttered by now with the rubbish of their activities and preoccupations unrelated to this secret treasure deep within them.

Others have a more constant awareness of their pool's actuality, but this awareness is distorted by their rigid habit patterns of thought and behavior that they cling to because they feel more secure with the familiar. These distortions provoke wrong ideas about the pool's nature and purpose, and even of its location, so that, in spite of good intentions, these seekers after security often take the wrong path and end up at the brink of some pseudo-pool. Mistaking it for reality, they settle down beside it for a lifetime, deluded but comfortable, and self-righteous in their delusions.

Still others are aware of the pool and visit it conscientiously, caring for it and doing their best out of a sense of duty to keep it pure and full. They do not realize that their dutiful approach lacks love and self-forgetfulness. They regard the pool as their own rightful possession and tending it as a matter of self-respect. When they are regular and punctilious in performance, they congratulate themselves on being so much better than the renegades who never come or are so remiss as caretakers. When they themselves become somewhat lax in their duties, they can always find clever, convincing rationalizations to excuse themselves.

In effect, they are more concerned to have a good opinion of themselves and show others that they are worthy pool-keepers, and that therefore their pool is more beautiful than those of others, than they are about the wonder, beauty and purity of the pool itself. In a strange way they are dissociated from it even as they are preoccupied by it and their relationship with it and how much they are busy about it.

There is another, rarer group. Its members are like the old woman in my story. They have such a grace of awareness of the pool's nature and presence in them, its power to heal and sanctify, that they voluntarily choose to renounce much of what others consider makes life worthwhile. They do this in order to free themselves to be constantly and undistractedly by the pool, learning its wordless messages and striving always to apply them in their own lives and to pass on to others the riches being bestowed on them as a result.

They do this not so they can congratulate themselves, but to serve the pool's purposes and learn how to apply these to their own and others' lives. They are servants of the pool, not of their own aggrandizement, and as their faithful devotion is perfected through the years, they themselves take on the pool's qualities so that everywhere they go its holy powers are active within them and flowing out for anyone and everyone else's needs. Ruled by the one desire to serve the Master and their neighbor and become pellucid channels for the pool's waters, they are filled with diamonds and crystals of love and holiness.

The following chapters will be concerned with this final group, what makes them so compellingly beautiful, and how we can emulate them.

REFLECTIONS IN A POOL

You made this pool of silence
when your excavations climaxed,
pulverizing solid rock and tossing rubble
high into the air—a volcano
spewing up its magma.

I bled clay and pebbles, mud
and monolithic, Stonehenge slabs embedded in me
from past centuries of archetypal shaping—
the human ancestry that made me what I was.
I heard you muttering, "I must get rid of this. . . .
That will have to go. . . . I'll atomize
this mass of granite. . . . Right here
I'll sink a shaft to give me access
to those strata where I've stored
artesian waters pressing to spout free
from tiered, impervious seams of self-defense."

The excavation process, pitiless in purpose,
lasted convulsive years.

Then when
a cavern like a bomb's ferocious hole
was opened up and smoothed into the shape
you wanted (what I wanted was irrelevant)
you rested. It was your seventh day.

And after you had rested
you lifted high one stalwart, practiced arm
and cried aloud: "Flow, living waters!
Fill with your tranquil purity
this sculptured space.
Come, make a pool where I can gaze
upon my own resplendent face."

And so the waters surged from that concealed
artesian source. And I leaned over, peering
in the pool they formed, and saw
upon its limpid mirror surface
your celestial image,
and merging with it,
all a-glimmer, was my own.

The Prayer of Peace in the Depths

❧

This prayer arises from deep within the Pool of Tranquillity. It is able to do this because grace has dissolved away all obstructions preventing the free upwelling of the Spirit's strength and guidance. Now this influx occurs spontaneously whenever the Spirit moves deep down to activate the hidden wellsprings of the substrata and release their stored life-giving powers into the soul's pool.

The Spirit's action is like that in the biblical Sheep Pool in Jerusalem whose waters were "troubled" at various times, and when this happened, the sick who immersed themselves in the pool were healed. The Pool of Tranquillity has such immense healing powers, but it is necessary to be spiritually immersed in them in order to benefit. Immersion occurs only under certain conditions.

We must know the location of the Pool. We must be aware of its properties, have faith in them, long for the healing they can give, and be ready to discipline ourselves into receptivity. Then we must have the courage and perseverance to act when the Spirit, responding to our readiness, urges us to do so.

Jesus promised, "My own peace I give you, a peace the world cannot give—this is my gift to you" (Jn 14:27).

Jesus' way of bestowing peace, and the quality of that peace, can be so unexpected and even alarming that we involuntarily draw back from contact with it, for it means renouncing the ersatz peace the world gives. We may have found "peace" in possessions, riches, a satisfying career, a personal relationship, a psychological reorientation, a certain life-style, a particular philosophy, or even a special form of prayer.

The Lord's peace requires us to become detached from all these in order to open ourselves to his own everlasting peace and the fulfillment of his plan for us—not what we thought till now that plan entailed, but what it *is*.

And this may well be a complete mystery.

An essential part of peace in the depths is resting in mystery, content not to know, but just to accept.

Peace has been called "the tranquillity of right order," and the peace of Jesus bestows this. Right order consists of putting him and his plan for us first in our lives and personal relationships at all times.

During the active nights we have deliberately labored at casting out the rubbish from our lives and hearts, and in the passive ones have submitted to the Spirit's action in the deepest areas we ourselves could not reach. We have been "cleared"—the detritus got rid of. As a result our inner house is now in order, and peace reigns. As John of the Cross puts it in the first verse of *Dark Night:*

> I went forth without being observed,
> My house being now at rest.

Roy Campbell's translation reads:

> Upon a gloomy night,
> With all my cares to loving ardours flushed,
> (O venture of delight!)
> With nobody in sight
> I went abroad when all my house was hushed.

In this "hushed" house, where all is "at rest," there is no commotion of warring elements, with "I want" furiously opposing God's "This is what *I* want for you." Things are in their right place, and we know where they are, so we do not have to fumble about looking for them in a state of confusion.

One aspect of right order in a house is knowing you will put your hand on what you need exactly where you expect to find it. Nothing in this house is any longer out of alignment. The foundations are firm and earthquake-proof. The walls are impregnable. Every angle is true. Things stay where they are put, and they are always put in their proper places.

The whole house is clean, light and airy. The perfect order present in the Trinity's own circumincession becomes ours too, since at last we are wide open to receive it flowing into and through us. There is harmony and cooperation among the parts—mental, psychological, emotional, instinctual, spiritual—of our inner self. No burglars or vandals can break in and desecrate this house, for the Lord himself is the rampart around it. One of Satan's trademarks is destructive chaos—like Berlin after the blitz. He can no longer gain entry to this dwelling place through any crack or underground tunnel or loose tiles in the roof in order to wreak havoc, for Christ reigns undisputed here, and he is Lord of All.

In the passive purgations the unconscious was bit by bit infiltrated by the benign influences of the Spirit, and where the Spirit of God is, there is peace and harmony. The unconscious has not been annihilated, but rather blessed into a quiet restfulness. The violent emotional eruptions of the cleansing and purifying processes no longer occur. Now, when it sends up its "messages," they have come through the Spirit, acting as a kind of filter, as it were. They register on the intuition by means of "substantial touches." They are like the upwellings in the Pool of Tranquillity.

The substance of the soul is its deepest core, or depth, or ground, that yet has no material constituents. It is this that the passive purgations of the spirit have penetrated and cleansed and so made capable of receiving the Spirit of Love in transforming union. It is now transformed in God and subject to the Spirit's guidance in the manner and to the capacity that God ordained for it when he created it. This is like a return to "original innocence."

Through infused acts that meet no barrier of self-interest, God now often produces instantaneous, intuitive understandings, so that we see things "whole," without having to split them up into component, intellectual parts. Like the whisper of God to Elijah, these touches of loving wisdom are usually gentle, subtle, delicate, sure and profoundly convincing.

It is indeed certain that the Spirit has produced this inner tranquillity and continues to guide its expression in our lives. Compared with the turmoils and sufferings of the past earthquake-like adjustments, this peace is almost incredible, yet it is undoubtedly both real and operative. "For the time being, all correction is painful rather than pleasant; but afterwards, when it has done its work of discipline, it yields a harvest of good dispositions, to our great peace" (Heb 12:11).

These past "corrections" occurred because God is by nature the enemy of our self-love and self-will, and hence of all those deeply ingrained tendencies to sin, and all the gross imperfections and faults in a nature wounded by the first syndrome. It was God's holiness as contrasted with our sinfulness that we experienced as bent on annihilating us. In reality, of course (though we could not at that time register it as such), this purgative action was the refining, living flame of his love burning up the dross to make it possible for us to enter into final love-union with the Trinity.

The abrasive action of his purpose was intent on wearing away "the foul, stinking lump of sin" inherent in us, but we could not help recording it as a cruel determination to scour us out of existence. His healing power was invading the very roots of our crippledom to heal us and make us straight and strong, as Peter and John, in the name of Jesus, made the crippled man. Now we go spiritually, "walking and jumping and praising God," where before we could only crawl and endure, or maybe were incapable even of doing that.

Our self-love violently resented the efforts of perfect Love to make us whole and transmute us into aspects of himself—free, strong and at peace in him. It was our own opposition, fear and inability to submit to the healing process that made his love seem like hate to us.

Now that our inner caverns have been cleared of the bogies, there is peace in their depths. In the blessed stillness after the storms, nothing ominously threatens to boil up and over in the equivalent of a volcanic eruption. The now extinct volcano has itself become our Pool of Tranquillity.

In this inner peace we are conscious of integration and wholeness. The parts all fit together, and they have meaning and a sublime message like an exquisitely complex yet somehow fundamentally simple mandala. Everything is inter-related, and the former painful sense of fragmentation has vanished.

This is a house which is truly functional, its rooms leading one into the other and perfectly adapted to their various purposes. At the center of the house is its power source—God's all-embracive will, the Spirit's action, and our love-union with the Beloved, who is the Lord of Glory. At this source is a pivotal Christ-consciousness rather than self-consciousness, and from it flows "the peace that passes all understanding." There will never be power cuts now in this house, for it has become the permanent dwelling place of the Trinity.

Everything functions so smoothly and artlessly that we realize the aperture of consciousness has been widened so we can receive the grace of heightened awareness. Under its influence we see clearly the divine purpose and how it interlocked all aspects and happenings of both our past and present existence. Everything is integrated, and the prayer of peace in the depths flows from our serene awareness that God is All in all, and always has been, only in the past we were afflicted with blindness and rebellion.

Recollection and simplicity of will are particular graces of this state. The will is no longer battered about in a house at war with itself and God's will. "You keep him in perfect peace whose mind is stayed on you, because he trusts in you" (Is 26:3), or, as Dante very simply puts it, "In his will is our peace."

What was formerly apt to be "free-floating anxiety" has become "free-floating in endless love," trusting it and effortlessly accepting as best whatever it presents to us at each moment. Peace is the fruit of resting uncomplainingly in the sacrament of the present moment, certain that God knows what he is doing, even if it is presented to us under unattractive disguises. It is a state of having relinquished the past, of not reaching out for the future, of saying "yes" to the here and now. Once everything can be accepted as from the hand of an infinitely loving and caring God, then peace in the depths results, because trust is perfected.

"I have been through my initiation and now I am ready for anything anywhere—full stomach or empty stomach, poverty or plenty. There is nothing I cannot master with the help of the One who gives me strength" (Phil 4:12-13).

Through acceptance and abandonment coupled with the Spirit's penetration, both down from the upper layers of consciousness and will, and up from our deepest depths in the artesian sources of the living waters, we are cleansed. The combined inflowing and upwelling process of grace's action can now accomplish, because of our openness and trust, what it wants to in us and in our lives. It can also issue unchecked from us to be a beneficial influence in others' lives, material and spiritual.

This peace in the depths of transformed souls is a most potent force for world peace, because it is directed at the inner realities of problems, the motives and secret urges of people known only to God, rather than at materialities produced from them.

"To the victor I will give the hidden manna" (Rev 2:20). In this instance the hidden manna is the positive spiritual force of love and peace that issues from the Christed soul and far surpasses in power the negative, destructive force of evils such as nuclear fallout or invisible, death-dealing viruses. Of course, to believe this is the fruit of heroic faith and trust, and it is the very intensity of this heroism that produces the power in which good overcomes and destroys evil. "This is the victory over the world, our faith" (1 Jn 5:4)—the faith that can move mountains.

Once there is peace in our depths, the famished longing for God that formerly tortured us is replaced by the serene certainty of his ceaseless presence, plus a sense of being constantly, intravenously fed. This is a fixed state that remains intact under all surface fluctuations. It is unrelated to them and free from their disturbing influence because it arises from the uninterrupted, permanent love-union with Jesus that is of the essence of spiritual marriage. It is part of the established communion with the risen Christ (rather than with his passion–crucifixion–entombment cycles) that denotes the presence of both the third syndrome and resurrection love-life. A quiet, persistent happiness and sense of blessedness permeates our whole existence. This graced state is dependent not upon any outer circumstances, but upon the permanent, interior presence of the Lord, of which we are now experientially certain.

"Even in this world we have become as he is" (1 Jn 4:17). Christ is our center of repose, the Master of our inner house of rest and peace. Having cleared a space for himself within us, with our full, willed acceptance of all the pains of that reorientation, he now pours his own attributes of holiness, love and peace into us, so we may have treasure to give him. Christ in our earthenware vessel transforms it into the richest, most precious elements and adorns it with himself. "We are only the earthenware jars that hold this treasure, to make it clear that such an overwhelming power comes from God and not from us" (2 Cor 4:7).

This transfigured earthenware pot has become his "secret place [where] he speaks his peace," and "the sooner [the soul] reaches this restful tranquillity, the more abundantly does it become infused with the spirit of Divine wisdom which is the loving, tranquil, lovely, peaceful, sweet inebriator of the spirit" (*Living Flame*).

BORN AGAIN

I realize from my time among you in the flesh
that your body's weakness dare not view
my unveiled glory. Like the flash
from nuclear explosions you have devised
to kill or maim so many of our family
it would blind and melt your human eyes.

So I take pity on you and conceal my presence
in your secret inner heart. Even it shrinks back
as love invites it to unclench and make a place for me.
But when you let me in as to my home we find
such mutual delight that all your flinching
turns into felicity, a fleshless two-in-one.

And so my plan in being born of woman
is fulfilled. I dared to sow my seed
in your half barren heart, but scarcely hoped
for harvest half as rich as this. Do you recall
our Golgotha? You shared it all with me—
you heaved and sweated, bled and died with me.

Then afterward we lay entombed together. That proved
your love. To even dare the grave with me
revealed you truly faithful to the end.

My good seed had taken root and now
a mighty tree has sprung from it. Who knows
how many birds you'll shelter in your widespread boughs?

I love you. Do you understand the implications?
Now that both of us have left the tomb behind
and you are born again in the new life I bestow
on my beloveds, I long for you to share my glory.
Here, shelter in my arms against my heart.
I'll shield your human eyes with my pierced hand.

SUNRISE BEFORE THE CAVE

Eve,
I love you when you are so quiet,
when stillness takes possession of you
and you sit composedly upon that ancient stone
Adam placed where he could see the ocean.
When your hands no longer
beat the air in passionate protest, but
folded in your lap, stay there quiescent. When
your grey, far-seeing eyes, now translucent,
gaze in wondering worship at the rising sun.

Eve,
I love to sit beside you then and share
the blessed moment, consummate
our ancient partnership in peace, not war.
I touch your hand in reconciliation.
You do not edge away. Instead
you turn and look at me
and in your eyes I find
shy recognition that we two
are soul friends, consecrated twins.

Glorious Liberty

To be free is one of the basic human hungers. Bondage afflicts us in so many ways—living under a tyrannical political system; in exile or in poverty or imprisoned; trapped in a misery-provoking marriage, or incurable illness, or way of earning one's living; afflicted by some humiliating psychosis, neurosis, compulsion, obsession, moral weakness, emotional need. . . .

The forms of loss of liberty are innumerable, and all of them are crucifying to our fundamental need for freedom and fulfillment. Yet all can be endured, even heroically, if the sufferer has strength of character and an intensely meaningful philosophy of life.

Spiritually, freedom and slavery are related to sin.

Either we are in slavery to sin, or we are set free from it in the power of the risen Christ. Baptism is an act of liberation that precipitates us into a new life in which we are "dead to sin but alive for God in Christ Jesus." When, usually after years of struggle and sacrifice, we become fully one with the risen Lord in his love-life of glory and freedom from entombment, we realize that we are "living by grace and not by law."

Now we have been "freed from the slavery of sin" precisely so we could "become slaves of righteousness." Baptismal grace has finally reached its destined fulfillment in us. To become a joyful slave of God, permeated by Trinitarian love-life, is to be graced into freedom and God's gift of "eternal life in Christ Jesus our Lord" (cf. Rom 6).

Those who are literal slaves to other human beings are forced to be abject and humiliated. They can be sold at their owner's whim. They must always submit without demur to another's will and perform whatever task is set them. They are subject to abuse, cruel punishment and even death if they disobey or show rebellion in any way. Even a good master still treats them like objects, not as persons with individual rights and a life of their own.

With us, the baptized, it is different. Once we have been deeply cleansed, not just of outward sins, but of the very roots of sinful tendencies, by the power and grace of God won for us by Jesus, we enter his own resurrection love-life and share his own freedom.

"Everyone moved by the Spirit is a son of God. The spirit you received is not the spirit of slaves bringing fear into your lives again; it is the spirit of sons and daughters, and it makes us cry out, 'Abba, Father!' The Spirit itself and our spirit bear united witness that we are children of God. And if we are children we are heirs as well— heirs of God and coheirs of Christ, sharing his sufferings so as to share his glory" (Rom 8:14–17).

This glorious liberty of the sons and daughters of our Abba-God is entered into stage by stage as we learn to live out in all their fullness our baptismal promises and benefit from the new life infused into us through that sacrament.

First we have to understand and be repelled by the enormity of sin and what it has done to the human race and our planet earth since our first deviation from primal blessedness. Where and exactly how this happened, we cannot know. That it happened, and has continued to evince itself in innumerable appalling ways ever since, is revealed plainly in the Bible and any history book.

Scripture shows us why and how Jesus released us from our collective slavery to sin, and what the consequences of our liberation were and are. To read Acts and the letters of Paul and his associates is to encounter a concept of freedom far surpassing that of the material liberty of literally freed prisoners and slaves.

What Jesus and his followers teach is an inner, everlasting, incorruptible liberty that comes to us through his gift of his own eternal life. This resurrection love-life streams into our hearts through the Spirit. It fills us wherever we make inner space for it by renouncing sin down to the innermost, deeply secret strata of our human will, innate drives and disguised desires and hungers.

When at last we are both cleared and cleaned, we resemble, spiritually speaking, the Pool of Tranquillity in its limpidity and unobstructed openness to the upwelling living waters whenever they choose to become active.

Entering resurrection love-life is like being let out of prison, like the stone being rolled away by an angel and there at the mouth of our stifling tomb in the rock are light, fresh air, the sun, freedom.

It is like John of the Cross's dog that runs pitifully and ceaselessly to and fro on its tether (which represents our compulsive attachments to the not-God), and then unexpectedly the rope is cut, so that the animal bounds away, reveling in being loosed.

It is like wakening at first light after a night of agony in a sickbed where there was no one to help you. Now the turning point has come, the fever has vanished, the window is wide open, the clear, clean air is flowing in to refresh you, the dawn chorus is resounding. Rejoicing, you know the sun will surely rise, and today you, too, will rise from your sickbed to sit by the open window and feel the sun's warmth and a gentle breeze on your face again.

It is like having been completely separated from your dearest love for years. (Perhaps he has been in a prisoner-of-war camp.) You have remained faithful, but there has been no communication, and your heart has never stopped grieving. Then you look out the window one day and there he is hastening up the path, laughing with joy to see you. You race toward each other, and in his ecstatic embrace you know that at last you are safe forever.

Entering resurrection love-life makes us like the apostles after the Holy Spirit had come down upon them at Pentecost. All in an instant the risen Lord is an experiential presence in our own hearts and lives. We want to "go out to the whole world and proclaim the good news" that he is indeed risen. His radiance permeates us, his exultant entry into eternal life is drawing us after him into felicity. An ocean of fulfillment passes from him to us, and we are immersed in it, part of him. Since it is he who has made us free, we are free indeed. Till now we have been unable to understand the true meaning of the phrase "the glorious liberty of the daughters and sons of God." Now we are living in it.

God first loved us, before ever we came to be, and through experiencing that love in a personal relationship with him, we learn how to love him, ourselves and others. We are released into love. Nothing any longer inhibits our expression of it, and we offer it in full awareness of its Source. Such awareness, coupled with the freedom to be an open channel for the gift of love, is a sure sign that the grace of glorious liberty has been received, nurtured and understood for what it is, and that we have been assigned the task of passing it on.

In resurrection love-life's glorious liberty we experience Christ as Love incarnate, and the necessity and purpose of his redemptive sufferings are made plain to us through the Spirit's infused graces and gifts. We are open and free to receive these as never before, because out of our love for Jesus and our fellow human beings we have for many years willingly shared his passion with him in the active and passive purifications. Now we are sharing his glorification.

"The love of Christ overwhelms us" as we consider the incredible weight of sin that he accepted and bore for our sakes "so that in him we might become the goodness of God" (cf. 2 Cor 5). The mystery of redemption is revealed, and we long to be merged with him in a dynamic empathy of total sharing, our wills fused with his.

This lack of recoil from the personal implications for us of Christ's sufferings is one of the signs of full union with him. Perfect Love has cast out fear and we are now free to go, be, and do whatever the Lord wants of us. We see the glory on the face of the risen, liberated Savior, and it gives stupendous meaning to the tortured face of the Crucified.

"When Christ freed us, he meant us to remain free" (Gal 5:1). He also expects us to make use of that freedom by paradoxically becoming, with Paul, his slave. Then we are not any longer the slave of any human being, through being driven by our own needs and hungers to center our life on that person, to the detriment of choosing first to belong to God and letting our human relationships, of whatever kind, flow out from our union with him.

To be the slave of God is to enjoy perfect liberty, as those who have rendered up their whole selves and lives to him well know. It is also to put oneself unreservedly at his disposal for the sake of others, and this is another hallmark of the resurrection state of glorious liberty.

"So though I am not a slave of any man I have made myself the slave of everyone so as to win as many as I could. . . . I made myself all things to all men in order to save some at any cost" (1 Cor 9:19, 23).

Now our "inner man is renewed day by day" (2 Cor 4:16) and minute by minute, because we are "in" Christ's resurrection love-life, and "there is a new creation" within us, making us constantly aware that "now is the favorable time, now is the day of salvation" (2 Cor 5:17; 6:2).

"Through faith we [have] received the promised Spirit" (Gal 3:14). We are baptized into and clothed in Christ, who, himself finally fulfilled and freed from all earthly limitations, invites us to participate in his Trinitarian liberty. Essentially, this is freedom to love. God is love, and once we are placing no barrier, deliberate or involuntary, between ourselves and Love, it possesses us, pouring out through us for the world. Now we have also entered fully into our individual personhood, becoming what we were created to be, other Christs, showing forth his resurrection love-life and finding in it our own predestined fulfillment.

To be genuinely fulfilled is to be free of all frustrating limitations. Now we are able to choose to be and act as we truly want, part of his extended incarnation and a participant in his redemptive love-gift of himself.

In whatever way this love-gift, under the direction and inspiration of the Spirit, expresses itself, the core disposition of the donors is the same. Rooted in the indwelling Trinity, it blossoms and fruits in a myriad different ways adapted by the Spirit to our individual life circumstances, temperaments, strengths and shortcomings. There is no boring mass production of those in the state of glorious liberty, but the power behind their multifarious ways of expressing resurrection love-life is the same—God's love poured out into their wide-open hearts through his Spirit.

Only divine love has the power to free us into its own ineffable capacity and will to give without the need to reserve something for oneself, but instead in joyful self-immolation.

We are now enabled to receive from the Spirit whatever special vocation or mission for the church and the world is God's choice for us. This may be made plain to us in one flash of illumination, or be gradually clarified over a quite lengthy period. With the mission is given the grace to fulfill it and the perseverance to persist no matter what the setbacks. There is a deep sense of having found our true métier and a fundamental satisfaction in acting to bring it to fruition. The way opens, and though a variety of obstacles may appear in it, somehow they are overcome through the power of grace.

Part of glorious liberty is the ability to receive and be guided by intuitions directly infused by the Spirit. These give a sense of unerring direction and of communion with divine Wisdom far transcending any derived from human intellectual weighing of pros and cons, though these have their uses. We are free to be completely protected by God's providential will, which, though it may not keep us from suffering and setbacks, yet safeguards us in the essential way Jesus meant when he said not a hair of our head would be harmed.

It is rather like having had arthritically crippled hands that are now healed so that we can fit the power plug swiftly and accurately into the power socket, and pull it out again easily, with the anticipated, immediate results. Before, we were hampered by clumsy, twisted, weakened, swollen joints and fingers, and perhaps also by a power point that was itself defective, or by other factors such as a power failure, or by not being able to find the socket in the dark. Now all that is gone and we are free to use the mechanism accurately and in accordance with its design. Our fingers function as they are meant to, and so do the plug and its socket.

There is right order through our whole being, and we no longer bruise our shins and fall and break an arm through stumbling against harmful obstacles and the rubbish of unfinished business and restless desires left lying about. We are able to move uninhibitedly and safely in the direction we have chosen under the Spirit's guidance. Our inner house is in order.

The final fulfillment resulting from the long purifications of love is the work of the Holy Spirit (who has instigated, inspired and shaped the whole process). Traditionally it has been called "spiritual marriage" or "transforming union." This is the supreme peak experience and summit of both resurrection love-life and the third syndrome. Now we are indissolubly one with the Trinity. We are given an awareness of this as a fact—though not usually in any extraordinary way. Our awareness may be little more than a quiet, absolute certainty that God is within, that we are uninterruptedly penetrated by his presence, that he will never leave us now, that we are at last gloriously free in our consent to be possessed and used by him however he chooses. "I am my Beloved's, and he is mine."

Our certainty that the indwelling is a living force within us is final and indelible.

John of the Cross writes sublimely of this state of full union in *Living Flame of Love* and *Spiritual Canticle,* but people do not necessarily experience it ecstatically, or in the manner he describes. Its essence is the perfection of infused faith, hope and charity, and their heroic practice in great peace of heart, the peace of God that passes all understanding.

> Our life, like a bird, has escaped from the snare of the
>   fowler.
> Indeed the snare has been broken and we have escaped.
>   (Ps 123)

TABOR

"Come up higher," you said. "I can't!"
I panted, hoping you would understand
my weaknesses and fear, my dread of heights.

"Come! I'm telling you!" My lungs
were bursting from the lack of oxygen.
My eyes were aching with the glare of snow,
my body in every muscle, bone and limb
yelled with decisiveness, "No! I can not,
will not, climb another step!"

*   I glimpsed*
a glory and a dazzle on the other side
of that bare, ultimate peak that soared
against cerulean skies. You goaded me.
I cried out, "No! You ask too much!

I'm only human. You make
impossible demands. Don't you understand—
I can't go on! I'm beaten!"

                    You
smiled at me then—a half ironical
though cherishing smile that brimmed your eyes
with tenderness—so I capitulated,
set jaw and jellied legs and, roped to you,
I climbed and clung, groaned and half blacked out
until my fingers gripped that final saw-edged ridge
while I hung helpless in a panic void.

Your strong hands clamped my wrists. You hauled me up
to lie spread-eagled on my back upon
the summit's rocky ledge. I saw
infinity and cried out loud,
"The sky! The sky! It stretches on forever
filled with light! It brims with glory! I've arrived!"

Freed into the Floating Prayer

One way in which our glorious liberty expresses itself is through the floating prayer.

As the name which I have given it suggests, this prayer is the experience of spiritual weightlessness, in which we are freed from anything and everything that could impede our soaring into God. We spiritually levitate into his love. The floating prayer is the experiential awareness of this elevation.

To illustrate what I mean, I cite a personal experience, and, at the end of this chapter, some poems that have flowed from this and other similar graces.

It was autumn. The days were golden, rich with sun and warmth, the nights crisp. I lay on my back on the grass outside my caravan where I could glimpse the blue ranges, watch the movement of trees in the wind, hear the soft gurgling and shushing of the stream, the bleating of sheep, the many different bird calls.

Two fantails were engaged in complex aerobatics high above the stand of rimus. A kingfisher, in a startling flash of turquoise, sped across the stream. My dog Carla slept peacefully on her side nearby. I let my gaze wander in the spiky patterns of the huge pine's boughs and tufts of needles, the might of its rough, grooved trunk, the birdlife flicking and flitting in its branches.

This was my personal place of retreat where I came periodically

to be alone—except for Carla—with God, in silence, except for the
sounds of nature.

I looked at the sky. And there against the clear, sunlit blue was a
drift of thistledowns, scores of them, sailing serenely on the breeze,
their delicate, airy shapes filled with light, spinning and darting,
eddying and soaring, idling and dancing—all at the impulse of the
gentle wind. Entranced by their beauty, I was once more reminded
what a perfect symbol they were for the floating prayer. They were
attached to nothing. They did not choose where or when they would
move, but left it to the will and whim of the wind.

They were weightless, unimpeded by any kind of encum-
brance, their shape perfectly adapted to their function of floating.
Nothing about them opposed or rejected their airy environment.
Everything they were affirmed it. They were fragilely yet enduringly
beautiful. Eventually the wind would bear them to some landfall.
The air becoming still, they would drift down to the ground. Here
they would bring forth new growth.

As I watched, entranced, steeped in their symbolism, my spirit
was caught up with them, and I too floated—in God.

> All in a moment I became aware
> that, flightless, earthbound biped though I am,
> beyond that fleecy, shining, sunset cloud
> I floated, weightless in the pure air
> upheld by nothing but your will
> choosing to keep me airborne there.

Spiritually, the essence of the floating prayer is weightlessness,
indicating non-attachment to everything and everyone but God.
This means more, not less, loving, for in the state of being unen-
cumbered we love for the sake of God and the beloved, not for our
own satisfaction of complex, often unconscious needs.

There is a pitiful psychological state in which sufferers are
possessed by what is called "free-floating anxiety." In the floating
prayer the recipient is in a state of free-floating love. The love is
God's love, Christ's self-bestowal, the Spirit's limpid joy—these
permeate, possess and elevate their human recipient into another
dimension of being. If it should take the form of bodily levitation,

such outward manifestation is only a sign of the inner state of a person fully abandoned in selfless love to God's usage. It is here, hidden away with Christ in God, that the true, because wholly spiritual, levitation takes place. It is here that God raises the soul to the various levels of the floating prayer.

God's will for each of us is that we unreservedly give all of ourselves to loving both him and other humans. It is the reservations that keep us fastened to the ground and prevent floating, and the roots of the reservations are buried in our own inevitable self-love and self-will, the depths of which only grace can reach and eradicate in the deepest passive purgations.

In faith we now know and affirm that with God all things are possible, and that Jesus became incarnate in order to delete the impossible from our lives. His commandment to love is unconditional. Somehow we must fulfill it. We are enabled to do so only in his strength and grace, for we can do all things in Christ who strengthens us, and only he can liberate us from "the body of this death," as Paul proclaims in the most heartfelt terms.

If we consent to be "in Christ," we consent to be "in" the total Christ, to follow him wherever he leads, to suffer, love, die and be raised up with him—for it is not possible to obey him otherwise. Our human capacities cannot by themselves function at his level. They need and must have his gift of enabling grace. This is how the impossible becomes possible. To float we need to enter with him and in his strength into his state of doing always the things that please the Father.

As mentioned in the previous chapter, John of the Cross uses a powerful metaphor for the heart that is captive to its own self-seeking desires, urges and appetites. "But the other man loses everything, running to and fro upon the chain by which his heart is attached and bound; and with all his diligence he can still hardly free himself for a short time from this bond of thought and rejoicing by which his heart is bound."

This analogy reminds me of a farm dog I once saw chained to an overhead wire so that it could run to and fro along it, but not get free. Its restless activity was an expression of pitiful imprisonment. Such a restricting "bond of thought and rejoicing" can be established in relation to both people and things. A handy question to ask oneself is, "Whom, or what, other than God, do I feel I can't do without? That puts me in a panic when I think of and fear losing, whether it's her, him, or it?"

It is not the enjoyment of our treasures that is at fault, but our disproportionate stress upon possessing them, and the way we let it crowd our relationship with God into the background, and cripple our human relationships by making us evade involvement with others' needs lest demands be made on us that will distract us from concentration upon our obsession. If we are, paradoxically, to be free to go on "running to and fro" upon our particular chain, then we cannot have human beings getting in our way and tripping us up. So we evade any full and true commitment to them, together with the resultant demands made on us by them.

In the end, it is always God himself who liberates us—if we let him.

The process goes on and on, over and over, in a spiral pattern, or a wave-like rhythm of crests and troughs, or a mountain-climbing effort of laborious scaling of cliff-faces interspersed with the attaining of and resting on some plateau a little higher up. In our helplessness and sense of getting nowhere, we realize, in spite of our stubborn perseverance, that God and his grace are absolutely essential to us if we are to reach our goal of floating in his love. What we have to do is stay still more often, and let it happen as we blindly trust God, our Abba. He alone can and will arrange circumstances in the best way for leading us and others into that floating state of love-union with him that is our true longing and his declared will for us.

Once this state of active-passivity is attained, we have entered the floating prayer in its initial stages, though probably what we shall feel is that we are finally grounded, or drowned in some chasm on the ocean bed, or lost and groping in a nightbound desert, or have become a hopeless failure in what we had thought of as our "spiritual life."

Paradoxes abound here, and to be in fact starting to float, when one appears to oneself to be earthbound, is one of them. Involuntary imperfections, faults and attachments do not hinder spasmodic and incomplete floating, though they do prevent the final soaring that comes in the state of glorious liberty. They are ropes, or perhaps just strings, partially tethering us to the ground. Various degrees and forms of floating are granted the committed lover before the end fulfillment, but for some time they will not be permanent.

I think of the mooring ropes holding the floating basket balloon, or the dirigible, to the ground. These are loosed gradually, until the craft is finally and completely airborne. Or I think of the gull or eagle fledgling learning to use its wings. It flips and flops about, succeeds in flying a little, is grounded once more, tries again with more success, and finally spreads those wings given by God for flight. Then it is caught up in the air currents and thermals so it soars majestically, gliding effortlessly, in its element at last.

John of the Cross writes in *Dark Night:* "By this mystical theology and secret love, the soul continues to rise above all things and above itself, and to mount upward to God. For love is like fire, which ever rises upward with the desire to be absorbed in the center of its sphere."

The paradox is that total commitment to God's will and abandonment to its action in our lives at last leads to a liberating "enslavement" instead of the demeaning one of running to and fro on our particular chain. This enslavement to God frees us to some degree and in this life into the unendingness of eternity and infinity where we float in his fathomless love, safe forever. Having tasted this brand of freedom, we are determined never again to do anything to destroy it. We now have the spiritual weightlessness of not clinging to anything God has created, but only to him, in whom we are finding, purified and glorified, all else that we have loved and cherished.

At last we gain insight into what Francis de Sales meant in his dictum, "Ask nothing; refuse nothing; desire nothing." And as we are given the grace of penetrating and living its meaning and implications more fully, we are lifted into more exalted heights of free-floating, for as long as we are in this life it is possible to grow in holiness and union with God.

The inward flight of the spirit denoting the floating state can occur though we have no more clearly defined awareness of it than a brief period of limpid peace; a sense of the divine Presence permeating us as surely as water does a sponge; a certainty that "all shall be well, and all manner of thing shall be (and is right now) well"; a realization that a river of love emanating from Jesus is pouring through us for others and that they sense this and respond; burning gratitude for all the graces bestowed, past and present, and a consequent experience of profound blessedness . . .

These are all intimations of the Spirit's deep penetration into our inner being, and of our being released to float in the divine indwelling. Occasionally there may be an experience that seems ecstatic in its intensity, but usually the floating is quiet and almost imperceptible. This is the best way for it to be, for then faith, hope and love are at their purest.

In this state the Spirit reveals the pattern divine providence has used to bring about these ends willed by God. We are shown how and why everything did and had to happen exactly as it did. We see clearly that what at the time appeared evil or tragic, and perhaps was temporarily and partially so, has been turned through the purpose and power of God into a means of achieving final good.

As a result of this insight we are able to let go of the urge to arrange our lives in the way that seems best to us, as if we knew better than God. We thus cut the last of the ropes preventing the balloon from lifting freely into space. Now we are able to leave the arrangements for our sky voyage to him, content to let him perfect his will in us and our lives according to his omniscience. This does not mean we succumb to inertia, relinquishing responsibility for our own lives and all power of choice. We do what is needful, but we trustfully leave the results of our actions in our Abba's care.

We do the best we can with the clearest light we have, turning over the results to God. If we have made wrong choices in good faith, we know he will bring a beneficial result out of them in his own way and time if we wait patiently upon his will. Jesus said, "When I am lifted up, I will draw all people to me." He has lifted us up to float with him in his ascension and resurrection state, absorbed into the divine will and love. Now nothing can ever harm us in any essential way again.

FLOATING FREE

1   Song of the Wings

The wings that stretched the heavens like clouds
I climbed upon. And long
and ardently they bore me in their easeful flight.
They were strong.
Tireless they were. I was a puny burden,
no more than dust.
The long, smooth surge I rested on became
my final trust.

The heavens' span and all the wide, thronged space of universes
is to these wings
an habitable room, a navigable place for leisured tours
and comfortable journeyings.
Now that I have cast myself upon their strength
what have I to fear?
And yet my heart is humbled into awe
to be so near.

2   Song of the Thistledown

I have no purpose but to float.
If you watch carefully you will see me
gossamer white against the sun,
my multitude of tiny aerials spread
so I can drift and spin
at the whim of the wind,
at the will of the Other's delight.

I float. That is my work. That
is what I choose to do.
I float.

Caught and tossed, I soar in an updraft.
I whirl, I dance, I spiral.

Stripped of waywardness,
freed from giddy desire,
I vanish deep into that Other
who permeates my airy habitat with love.

In stillness I turn in slow motion.
I am wafted without weight or purpose
in an eddy of light.

I have passed into felicity
forever.

   3   Song of Consummation

I lie in your cupped hands
quiet, still. The arching sky
is infinite above me. Clouds glide
serene as albatrosses
wind-borne from some bleak cliff
above the crashing waters.
You lift me higher, higher,
till I melt in ecstasy.

A life ago there was a girl-child
who lay upon a grassy hilltop
far from anyone, alone, aware of you,
gazing beyond the furthest reach of blue,
watching the filmy summer clouds sail by,
hearing the larks' filigree of trilling song.

You scooped her up into your blinding presence
and with one arrow of your love
marked out the route she was to take
through all the misty, unmapped years to come.

And now I have arrived. The consummation
surpasses anything that girl-child then imagined
and crowns her formless dreams with actuality.

FLOATING IN ENDLESS LOVE

Now nothing can entangle me.
In airy distances that have no end
I float. No mooring ropes
or strings, no thread of cotton
or even spider's silk
attempts to hold or hinder me. Unshackled
I dissolve in shoreless voids embracing all.

Eddies of your love flow round
and into me. They permeate
the unfleshed, boneless space I now inhabit
and gently actuate me here and there.
At times some mighty updraft
of your predilection makes me soar
far over Everests and stratospheres
and even stars, until I drift
into a maze of iridescent emptiness
brimming with you.

You play with me.
I am your partner in a cosmic dance
patterned and majestic, regal and controlled—
or else as artless as a child's
spontaneous gyrations in a swirl of joy.
Then I become a three-year-old
whose daddy, humoring her,
bows low and offers her his hand.
Laughing in glee, I cry, "More! More!" then suddenly
I go to sleep in trust within your arms.
Lulling me, you moderate the dance
until it glides with dignity and ease
among some distant, wheeling galaxy
while I sleep on in innocence and peace.

I am a thought you turned into a being,
an emanation of your endless love

you launched in time and space—
its impetus and destiny unique forever.

And now, in joyous swirling rush,
the convolutions of your love impel
my weightless self into infinity, and I,
a minute particle of you, never to be erased,
go spiraling like thistledown
soaring in a gale of ecstasy.

Your ruthless, ardent choice has put me here
and I have given you sole rights
to motivate me in this dance of love.
I would curtsy, pirouette and glide
exactly as your will dictates—
the plaything of your bliss.

                  I scarcely dare
to look upon the glory of your face
and yet my eyes can never stray again
now I am made your partner
in this floating pas-de-deux
of endless, liberating love.

The Prayer of Divine Indwelling

Grace comes to the believer in a multitude of ways, but awareness of the nature and reception of the various graces received is in itself a special and extra grace.

We believe in faith that we are temples of the living God as long as we are sacramentally united with him. The Trinity make their home in us if we do the Father's will, follow the Son faithfully, open our hearts to receive the Spirit, and love one another in Christ. This is basic Christian doctrine—and yet experiential awareness of God's presence within comes rarely in a clearly defined way. Most of our journey in faith is precisely that, and often it is a matter of stumbling in varying degrees of darkness along an ill-defined path between a precipice on one side and a soaring, insurmountable rock face on the other.

In the third syndrome we still continue in faith, but there is some light on the path, and our trust is so deeply centered in God that we are conscious of our feet being guided by the Spirit away from all hazards and straight toward our goal of full love-union.

The traditional doctrine of the indwelling of the Trinity, as expounded by Jesus at the last supper in John 13–17, is lived more and more fully as we mature toward this union. Once we receive the grace of resurrection love-life, it feeds on itself, as it were, till the moment of death, its splendor being enhanced with every act of love and abandonment.

Awareness of the indwelling varies greatly according to the

depth of our faith, hope and love and the kind of graces the Spirit brings us. The reality is concealed in the substance of the soul, motivating our whole life second by second through the Spirit's subtle guidance. Here we are hidden away with Christ in God even while we continue efficiently with our surface life. It is as if we are continuously held fast in the Father's loving embrace, but the degree of closeness is in relation to our own one-pointedness. Voluntary attachment and clinging for satisfaction to any created person or thing will lessen its intensity.

"In this soul wherein dwells no desire, image, form, affection for anything created, the Beloved dwells most secretly, with more intimate, interior and closer embrace, because the soul is completely withdrawn from all save God" (*Living Flame*).

God commands, "Thou shalt have no other gods but me." Our tendency to deify what he has created and make it the motivating force of our lives, rather than him, has been quelled and redirected in the deeper passive purgations. Now at last we are able to obey God's basic directive.

In the indwelling he treats us familiarly as if we were his own home where it is his right to place things where he—not we—wants them and use them for his—not our—purposes. Once in the third syndrome we acquiesce fully and gladly in this arrangement, treating him not just as a guest, but as the owner-proprietor whose prerogatives are absolute. We rejoice to be unprofitable servants fulfilling our prime duty of obeying, loving and serving him through the power of the very graces he himself bestows.

What have we that we have not received?

We know the answer is, "Nothing," and at last our poverty is our wealth and joy.

In chapter IV of *Living Flame* John of the Cross writes of two states of the indwelling. One is when we experience the Beloved as sleeping within us. This coincides with a low level of conscious awareness—cf. Thérèse's "Jesus is asleep in my little boat," and she is content to leave him in peace there. The other is when the Beloved wakens and we receive the grace of heightened awareness and are pierced by the bliss of consummated union, so that we are "ever conscious of God resting and reposing within." He alternately sleeps and awakens in "this embrace with the bride in the substance of the soul" and we "habitually have fruition" of him. That is, we are always aware, though at levels varying from vague and shadowy to intense and brilliant, of the glory of the Presence within us. We are also aware that Jesus is not in us now as the crucified Lord, but as the risen, glorified Son of God. We have "spiritual fruition" of him, but, as our Bridegroom, he seldom wakens fully, for if we had total awareness all the time of the blissful reality of the indwelling, we would already have died and would be in heaven. The term for this is "seeing God face to face," whereas now we see "a dim reflection in a mirror" (1 Cor 13:12).

At times of awakening "the soul is conscious of a rare delight in the breathing of the Holy Spirit in God, in whom it is glorified and enkindled in love." It is God himself who is "the sole cause" of these awakenings and blisses of full union in what is often termed "spiritual marriage," and so they are never tainted by our own self-seeking, but are divine graces received by us in purity of intention. If we had not become capable of such purity, we would be unable to receive them.

God now loves himself in us with his own love, and, for us, his channels and conduits, it is glad fulfillment to be used in this way. It is also balm for old wounds caused by our former barriers (voluntary and involuntary) against the inflowing of God, and that he had in some cases to tear out of us, they were so deeply embedded. Now they are all dissolved away by grace.

The intimate sweetness of being so abandoned to the divine usage and of experiencing oneself as being looked upon with such unutterable love during the awakenings is overwhelming.

God's presence at such a depth and completeness gives an enduring sense of "harmony, heavenly harmony," of absence of the slightest discord as our unequivocal "yes" meets his reaching out for the fullness of embrace. We are aware that, in a way beyond the tinkering insufficiencies of the human intellect's grasp, the whole of creation is ordered harmoniously, and that our own deep soul, indwelt by the Three, is now in tune with it. Right order prevails within and without, for God, the King and Creator of all, lives in his home in us, and all his servants (our faculties and above all our will) obey him, moving in unison and harmony with his desires and plans.

This does not mean that we now have some all-inclusive intellectual understanding of God's ways and purposes. We still go on in
faith ("thick darkness to the understanding") but also in profound
trust that all is well, has been and will be well.

Evil exists, but it has been overcome by the Savior through his
sufferings, death and resurrection. We now perceive, through grace,
that the Three in us, and in all creation, tirelessly and perfectly work
to transmute that evil into its opposite, and inevitably succeed in
their aim, even if it takes centuries of our time.

When deep and active, the indwelling gives an awareness of the
Three resting in the utmost intimacy within our essence, the Real
"I" of us, the substance of our soul that God infused into us at our
conception and that will last forever. When he chooses, he touches
this inner essence, causing it to become incandescent and immersed in his glory. This touch is very delicate, coming always in the
right manner and at the right time, while provoking our full consent
and response. It is also infinitely tender, healing all wounds.

It cures our spiritual blindness, so that we perceive the divine
presence in other people, and a new reverence for and appreciation
of them results. As he touches and embraces us, God is saying, "Let
me love them through you. Let me use you to touch and heal them,"
and our whole heart responds, "Yes! Oh, yes!" We see them with his
eyes as infinitely lovable and precious.

These touches reveal to us how we and all creation are one in
the Trinity and that the radiance of the divine face shines on all he
has made, purifying it and making it whole in him. He heals our
brokenness and glorifies us in his own glory. It seems as if, in the
very midst of the darkness of faith, our whole inner being is irradi-
ated by the glory of the indwelling risen Lord.

"And we, with our unveiled faces reflecting like mirrors the
brightness of the Lord, all grow brighter and brighter as we are
turned into the image that we reflect. This is the work of the Lord
who is Spirit" (2 Cor 3:18). Or as Ronald Knox translates it: "It is
given to us, all alike, to catch the glory of the Lord as in a mirror,
with faces unveiled; and so we become transfigured into the same
likeness, borrowing glory from that glory, as the Spirit of the Lord
enables us."

Only those who are in the resurrection love-life can bear this penetrating transfiguration of glory. It would burn up less purified souls, for it is the same fire as cleanses in purgatory and afflicts in hell. To be received and relished, it must meet and merge with (and indeed originate from) the infused glory emanating from the indwelling Three. If necessary, God puts a hand over our spiritual eyes, so his glory will not blind us. He shields us from too intense an impact from it, just as he did for Moses on Sinai.

This tender protectiveness is also one of the gifts of the indwelling. In the passive purgations we too often were afflicted by the experience of God as our destructive enemy. This was caused by the clash of his holiness with our sinfulness. But now every one of his touches is tender, and we are endlessly comforted and consoled by the unfailing gentleness with which he is looking after us, whatever the circumstances of our life, for these may still be adverse and even most painful.

This contradiction between inner and outer conditions is clearly exemplified by the martyrs who so often go to their usually horrible deaths in an ecstasy of loving abandonment to a divine will they know with certainty is an infinitely cherishing one.

Because God is now "closer than breath" to us, these touches are what John of the Cross calls "substantial"—that is, they reach and register on the deepest center or indestructible substance of the soul. Of course a soul has no physical dimensions, and such concepts are only metaphors, yet they do help understanding.

Since such touches are substantial, their effects are permanent, so that with each one divine grace beautifies and strengthens our inner being even more. It is as if the Spirit is grooming us so that we can glorify and please our spiritual Lover in every way. Each touch is a purifying encounter by which the Lover penetrates and possesses the soul more deeply than before.

"He penetrates the soul, continually deifying its substance and making it Divine, wherein the Being of God absorbs the soul above all beings. The reason for this is that God has encountered the soul and pierced it to the quick in the Holy Spirit . . . in order to glorify it quickly" (*Living Flame*).

The touches are both delicate and sublime, producing a sense of exaltation of the human spirit in the Holy Spirit, a lifting up with Jesus in his transfiguration. We know with certainty that it is impossible for this state to be self-induced, that only the Spirit could perform such a work, and that we are the humblest of humble, unworthy recipients. The soul surrenders itself in trust, wonder and boundless gratitude.

"He will build supernaturally in each soul the building that he desires" (*Living Flame*).

God wants his house to be just right for both him and us. It must fit the requirements of the two of us for eternity, and so he fashions it very carefully, both from the inside where he is already dwelling, and from the outside through the circumstances of our lives that induce us to persevere in practicing many virtues, but especially faith, hope and love.

We ourselves cannot build the house for his indwelling—we can only produce bricks that we offer to him and which he may reshape or discard, but always values if they are gifts of oblationary love. The house is built supernaturally, that is, by means of divine grace originating from him and bestowed gratuitously by him. Our role is to bring our pitiful bricks of efforts to please and serve him, and then let him get on with the job.

He is the master craftsman, we the humblest of day laborers. Through resurrection love-life he is able to work powerfully from where he already dwells within, and he shapes his habitation into a home that befits his splendor and our longings to be ever more and more intimately united with him.

There is one adequate contribution we are able to make at this stage where the indwelling is permanent, and that is to give God to God for him to use, with us as his means of expressing himself in time and space.

"They are sending back to God in God, over and above the surrender of themselves which they are making to God, since they are illumined and enkindled in God, those same splendors which the soul has received with loving glory. They turn to God in God, and become themselves lamps enkindled in the splendors of the divine lamps, giving to the Beloved the same light and heat of love that they receive" (*Living Flame*).

Jesus himself summed it up: "On that day you will understand that I am in my Father and you in me and I in you. . . . We shall come to him and make our home in him. . . . Make your home in me, as I make mine in you. . . . Whoever remains in me, with me in him, bears fruit in plenty, for cut off from me you can do nothing. . . . Father, may they be one in us, and you are in me and I am in you" (Jn 14:20, 23; 15:4, 5; 17:21).

INDWELLING

Where are you?
I keep feeling round in the dark
but I can't locate you. Once
I could hear you breathing
but now even that assurance is gone.
Is this some cruel game
you're playing with me?
Deliberately teasing me
because you're so sure that I'll stay faithful?

Well, after all these years
I'm an old hand at the game.
You can't deceive me.
I know you're there.
I'm absolutely certain
that you'll never go away.
We're bonded. Fused into one. Married.
And death won't part us—death will be
the final, time-and-space-transcending
absolute fulfillment of our mutual love.

So when I ask, Where are you?
I'm not really questioning,
for I know exactly where you are.

Here—inside me.
There—all about me.
Now—with every heartbeat and each breath.

Two in one flesh. No—
three in one flesh.
Heaven.
Here.
Now.
Everywhere.

The Prayer of Compenetration with Jesus

Another aspect of the indwelling is an especial awareness of Jesus himself, in all his mysteries, living and active within us. Once we are participating in his resurrection love-life, we experience him particularly in his risen and glorified state, but he also continues to live in and act through us as the whole God-Man. When he ascended, he did not leave his manhood behind him. He remains the incarnate Son forever, and that incarnation goes on expressing itself in time and space through us, the baptized.

Of all writers who have left their records of what it is like to live daily in Jesus in awareness that he is dwelling in us and we in him, perhaps Paul expresses the mystery most impressively.

In his initial, dramatic encounter with the risen Lord, it was punched home to him that Jesus identified himself with his church as with his own body. "Who are you, Lord?" "I am Jesus, whom you are persecuting." It was the infant church Paul had been so fiercely attacking, and here was Jesus saying, "I *am* the members of my church."

The message that Jesus identified himself with his members became the key element in Paul's teaching on the everyday life in

Christ of the believer. This inner reality was to be lived daily, moment by moment, through each believer's existential circumstances. Once baptized into Christ, there was no escaping him. He was everywhere all the time in one's life through his indwelling presence. Inevitably, he was also encountered living in others.

So fully did Paul merge himself with this inner Beloved that he could affirm, "Now I can live for God. I have been crucified with Christ, and I live now not with my own life but with the life of Christ who lives in me. The life I now live in this body I live in faith—faith in the Son of God who loved me and who sacrificed himself for my sake" (Gal 2:19–21).

By the time of the captivity letters, Paul's earlier sinful self had been crossed out by his sharing in Christ's crucifixion through sufferings endured for love of Jesus and the young church. He felt as if he was in labor with his converts until he brought them forth in Christ and they became as dedicated as he himself was. His own uninhibited identification with Jesus in all his mysteries had resulted in his being spiritually risen in him and operating apostolically in his power and grace. He had become fully confirmed in faith and lived by it as his physical body lived by air, water and food.

He had endured those deepest spiritual purifications by which the glorified Lord raises us to the exalted state of substantial, transforming union. Through his own resurrection love-life Jesus himself had taken over the management of his soul's house, living his life in and with him from this interior dwelling place that he foretold at the last supper, participating fully and permanently in all Paul's activities, directing every aspect of them through his Spirit. In this sublime manner the bond of sacrificial love uniting them was expressed through daily actuality.

The Jesus that Paul teaches is recognizably the Jesus of the gospels. Every word throbs with his real presence dynamically and personally experienced. Paul's awareness of the indwelling is constant and vivid. Because he literally "lives in faith," he is especially gifted in transmitting his belief to others. They "catch" it from him much as others "catch" a cold from someone else. His own life witnesses to it in a compelling manner, for he is continuously immersed in the prayer of compenetration and its impact drives him on to heroic self-sacrifice.

Paul has "put on Christ," and now the risen Lord is his environment. He lives and breathes Jesus, communes with and irradiates Jesus, exists in him as in his particular element as a fish does in its element of water. Removed from Christ, Paul would gasp and die, yet he knows this will never happen, for he is like an indelibly dyed garment—nothing can change his color now. Often he writes of being "transformed" and "transfigured" in Christ, and both his words and his actions demonstrate forcefully the effects that transforming union has on a human being once for all in love with Jesus.

Constantly he writes of being "*in*" Christ. In Ephesians he records that members of the infant church have received "all the spiritual blessings of heaven *in* Christ"; they have been personally chosen by the Father, not just at their conception, but "before the world was made." They were predestined to come into existence "*in*" Christ at an appointed time, so they could be "holy and spotless" emanations of the eternal Being, created for loving "*in* his presence." As adopted daughters and sons of the Father, they are to "praise the glory of his grace," given to them "*in* the Beloved"—not separately from him, but *in, with* and *through* him.

Made holy, and fulfilling their purpose "*through* his blood," they are, as an inevitable result, forgiven and released into spiritual freedom. Such great riches of grace poured out for them "*in*" Christ teach them the "mystery of his purpose" which he "made *in* Christ" at the beginning of time.

This all-embracing, awesome purpose, encompassing the whole of creation, and especially all humankind, was meant to unite them into one mystical whole, "under Christ, as head," and to be "*in* him . . . claimed as God's own, chosen from the beginning."

Chosen for what?

For God's "greater glory" and to "put their hopes *in* Christ." And now, being baptized *in* him, they have heard this "message of truth and the good news of their salvation, and have believed it."

Not only are they God's chosen, predestined, beloved daughters and sons in Christ the Son, but the Holy Spirit has put his seal on them, as "the pledge of their inheritance." Now they have an inconceivably holy destiny, in which—again Paul stresses it—they are meant, in freedom and grace, "to make his glory praised" (see Eph 1:3–14).

By extension, all this applies to each baptized person down through the ages who is born anew into the historical church.

Taken slowly, read and pondered over phrase by phrase, this passage holds depths of meaning and promise that cannot be understood through cerebration and natural reasoning, but only by means of the Spirit's infused insights and discernments—the "spirit of wisdom and perception."

Ephesians is perhaps Paul's sublimest statement on what I am calling "The Prayer of Compenetration," but the same message, basic to his whole doctrine, permeates all his teachings.

Such a life consists of the union of a human being and a divine one; a mystical communion of eternal Lover and time-and-place-bound beloved; an identification so intimate and all-embracive as to create one being out of two, and, by extension, one Being out of all who love and believe in the Lord who lives in each one of them. It is an actual identification of the Son of God with all those created for, and given to, him by the Father in the beginning of creation, and it results in the doctrine of the church being the body of Christ.

"If we live by the truth, and in love, we shall grow in all ways *into* Christ" (Eph 4:16).

"[Christ is] the head of the church, which is his body, the fullness of him who fills the whole of creation" (Eph 1:23).

"We are God's work of art, created *in* Christ Jesus" (Eph 2:10).

"And you too, *in* him, are being built into a house where God lives, *in* the Spirit" (Eph 2:22).

"Grow strong *in* the Lord, with the strength of his power" (Eph 6:10).

The Greek fathers spoke of our divinization in Christ and taught, "You exist in Christ." These are such startling and even terrifying notions that few ever face up to their full implications or seek to put them into practice. Consequently they do not enter into the fullness of resurrection love-life, which is essentially living constantly and deliberately in the whole Christ, incarnate, crucified, entombed, and risen. They evade the painful rebirth and re-creation, the putting back into right order what has been chaotically disordered, the dying on one level in order to live a new life on another. The dark night initiates and controls this process, but they are unable to let its final cleansings occur in themselves.

For those who do let themselves be immersed fully, the culmination is being able to say with Paul, "Life to me, of course, is Christ" (Phil 1:21). The crucial words are "of course." There is no alternative for Paul but to go the whole way. The call to union is imperative, and in his boundless generosity of self-giving, he can only answer, "Here I am, Lord. Send me." And he was indeed sent—over most of the then-known civilized world—to preach and teach a message that in essence was about living to the utmost degree *in and with* Christ. "It is for this I struggle wearily on, helped only by his power driving me irresistibly" (Col 1:29). He wanted everyone to reach the place where he was, a place of compenetration with the risen Lord.

Even his chains are "*in* Christ" (Phil 1:13). He is "crucified *with* Christ." Everything that most people cherish and seek after as necessary for a satisfying life is "so much rubbish" to him "if only he can have Christ" (Phil 3:8). In the midst of sufferings and privations he is glad to be "thought most miserable" when he is in fact "always rejoicing" (2 Cor 6:10).

All he wants is to "know Christ and the power of his resurrection and to share his sufferings by reproducing the pattern of his death" (Phil 3:10). He can say, "Life to me is Christ," and *in* Christ he shares *with* Christ every aspect of his Lord's experience and salvific mission.

The implications for us?

We enter the third syndrome and resurrection love-life through living each moment of our lives with and in Christ in conscious realization that he identifies himself with each of us personally.

This means a genuine sharing that does not repudiate whatever it is that Jesus offers. He cannot pray constantly in, with and for us through his indwelling Spirit unless we let him live the way he wants to in us and in our life circumstances. Both passivity to receive the messages and promptings of the Holy Spirit, and activity to carry them out faithfully with the help of whatever graces are offered, are needed.

Christ's prayer is essentially that the Father's will should be done through him in all ways and times, and at whatever cost to himself. As suffering Lord in us, this means that he calls us to share those sufferings, he in us, we in him. As risen Lord in us, he calls us to praise, glorify, thank and rejoice in each Person of the Three, and to worship the Godhead undivided, eternal, and ever-present in all creation.

He summons us to perfect abandonment. In such a state of trust we no longer put any obstacles, voluntary or involuntary, in the way of the triumph of God's plan in us, and through us for others. We are docile to the Spirit, and all our living is under its direction. We are quietly, unwaveringly certain that as long as we open ourselves and our lives fully to God's action, nothing but supreme good can come to us and to others through us. It may be a "disguised" good, but that does not alter its inherent quality, and in the third syndrome it is the latter we perceive and trust in.

Jesus is free to say in us, "I do always what pleases him," and "Behold, I come to do your will."

Since Jesus is living in us, we are aware always—though perhaps not consciously, for that is an extra grace—of his presence. Our constant prayer is expressed in our effort to live worthy of that presence. We know that his holiness is streaming into us. All we have to do is cooperate with its longing to flow out again to be part of his living waters fructifying and redeeming the whole world.

In order to be an open channel for him to use in this way, we need to be ever more closely made one with him. His prayer in us is, "Let me use you in my redemptive work," and our response is, "Use me, Lord, anywhere, anyhow, anytime. I belong to you."

Our own prayer is staying so close to him as to become indistinguishable from him in a state of compenetration. Then other people sense his presence in us and are drawn to him. We are meant to be compelling witnesses whose whole way of life and loving say, "Why look among the dead for someone who is alive? He is not in the tomb of my dead, sinful past life. He has risen in me. He lives in me in glory and grace and power. He wants to live in you if only you'll invite him in."

This is a kind of mirror prayer in which others see Jesus reflected in the mirror of our lives that are lived to his honor and glory.

In the compenetration prayer we constantly turn to Jesus, commune with him, share all our concerns, joys, hopes, fears, and sufferings with him. We talk to him, more often in the heart than in actual words. We listen for what he is saying to us. Our relationship is much like that of a happily married couple whose faithfulness has been tried, tested and found inviolable over many years. They know and accept each other so deeply that in fact they have little need for words, yet when they do talk together, they share their real selves and concerns. Each partner rests in the other, trusting and accepting without even being aware of doing so, because these attributes have become such a deep, unquestioning part of their relationship.

They know in their bones and blood that nothing and no one can ever come between them. Their love is so serenely wholehearted and reciprocated that they are certain that death, though it will part them physically for a time, will in fact be the doorway into their ineffable and eternal union. Though they have not in any way lost their individual identity, they have become one person.

So it is with the soul and Jesus in this state of compenetration where he has made his home in us so that we share absolutely everything and each moment with him. Nothing, now, can ever separate us from the love of Christ. He lives within us in an indissoluble union of committed, mutual love. One of its fruits is an exquisite sense of being cherished with the utmost tenderness. This balm heals every wound left by the piercings and obliterations of the spiritual passive purgations. "For I am certain of this: neither death nor life, no angel, no prince, nothing that exists, nothing still to come, not any power, or height or depth, nor any created thing, can ever come between us and the love of God made visible in Christ Jesus our Lord" (Rom 8:38–39).

THE VOICE

I was led down the path I had not chosen—
or, rather, I was drawn hypnotically.
One voice authoritatively announced,
"This is the way. Why do you linger? Move!"
Another seductively beguiled, "Don't listen."
It was the first I heeded. It gave me confidence.

Puzzling me, the signpost read, "Nothing and nowhere."
But the voice, now speaking in a foreign language,
urged me on. I recognized the intonation
though the words made nonsense. Then I asked myself,
"Who dares the wilderness alone, without a guide?"
And answered, "She who, hearing this discarnate voice, obeys."

The journey took me decades of hard labor.
"Here be wilde beestes" some old signs read.
Encountered in ravines, these snarling creatures sprang
to savage me, or growled and backed away
because they heard the voice cry, "Go!"
At other times they crouched to lick my feet and hands.

Some terrors of the way were sensed, not seen.
Atavistic panic seized me in the dark.
I quaked and sweated, froze and churned; the shadows
sparkled with malignant eyes, hooked claws and teeth
that gleamed—a nameless, faceless Thing. I flinched—
then heard the steely voice, "I order you—go back to hell!"

I got so that I could not believe this path—
obliterated as it often was by stones,
or halted like a crazy snake beside a precipice—
would ever lead me anywhere, and yet
I could not stop my legs' hypnotic motion
or my ears' compulsive listening for the voice.

And then one stygian night of deep, undreaming sleep
I heard it speak to me at last. Caress
of summer breeze was not more gentle. It said,
"Wake up, beloved. The long journey's over.
Open your bruised eyes, and gaze your fill of me."
I woke. I looked. I wept and laughed. I kissed my voice's mouth.

STORY OF A LOVE AFFAIR

He's saying to me, "What an unconscionable time
you took to get here! I've been waiting for so long!
What on earth kept you?"

                    I have to reply,
"in all sincerity" as they put it,
that it was indeed something "on earth"
that captivated me. For sixty-seven years
to be exact. It was love that made me late.

"Love?" he queries, laughing in my eyes,
just like any other lover. "But, dear heart,
I am Love. How could you possibly
be delayed by love when I am Love itself
who called and called you? Who kept waiting
and refused to give you up? So precious were you to me
that I pursued you everywhere you went
hypnotically repeating one word only, 'Come!'

"Sometimes I embellished it a little, calling,
'Come, my darling, come! Come to me, my love,
my dove, my fair one, come, come, come!'
Surely you heard me?"

                    I bow my head,
abashed. "I heard, but, Love—" "Ah!"
he interrupts, aglow with longing and delight.
"You called me by my name! You called me 'Love'!"

I want to weep and kiss his feet. I plead,
"Please listen. I must confess. I heard you—
but I became confused. It's true I knew
from the beginning that you were there,
and so I fell in love with Love
and was entranced, and sought you everywhere,

dazzled by the glimpses that you gave me
of your presence in my—oh!—
most precious and beguiling human loves.

"Did my astigmatic eyes see mirages?

"Reaching out to grasp them, I thought I'd found you
in the beauty that revealed itself to me.
I loved until it seemed my conquered heart
would burst asunder in its ecstasy.
I was so certain it was you I touched!
Beloved, I was sure!
How could it be that I was mirage-tranced?"

He smiles with such indulgent tenderness
that I begin to weep. One gentle hand
transforms my tears into a jewelled crown
and sets it on my head. His eyes are soft
with understanding pity. He draws my face
against his breast and murmurs in my ear,
"It was no mirage. I was there. Remember
I was human once and still retain
my humanness. I know what kind of beautiful
deceptive veils can interpose themselves between our eyes
and my eternal Beauty. I also know you sought me
without ceasing all your life, and yet
became confused at glimpsing me half hidden
in the one you loved, believing I was he.
Do not be troubled. You have found me now."

At last I rest where you have put me.
Your peace possesses me and in a swoon
I slip into my Love. Implanted then
within your Heart's wide wound
I lose myself in you and understand at last.

An Expert Witness on the Bridal Prayer

The seemingly extravagant statements of Jesus and Paul about the reality and effects of the indwelling and interiorized resurrection love-life are matched by those of the great experiential mystics, many of whom have left authentic, detailed records of what happened in and to them, and the consequent results in their lives.

As a Carmelite, though a secular, not an enclosed one, I am familiar and in tune with the spirituality of Teresa of Avila and John of the Cross, and in this chapter I draw on some of Teresa's writings about the characteristics of what is traditionally called "transforming union" or "spiritual marriage." In this book I equate these with full participation in the resurrection love-life of Jesus and with the love-joy-fulfillment syndrome.

First I emphasize some important facts, since the nature of these states is often misunderstood and misrepresented.

It is not extraordinary mystical and ecstatic manifestations and gifts that indicate an advanced degree of union and compenetration with the Trinity. The only reliable proof that the latter is present is the quality of a person's whole life—the heroic practice of virtue (especially love), the presence and action of the Holy Spirit and the accompanying gifts, and the perfection of abandonment to God's will.

Extraordinary manifestations may be given at any stage of the spiritual life as a special help over a difficult period, as a sign of predilection, or to convince others that here is one whom God has chosen for some special apostolate (for instance Paul's sublime revelation on the way to Damascus and Moses' vision of the burning bush). They may also arise from natural psychological or emotional traits, from delusion, or from a tendency toward over-dramatization and attention-seeking. And they can even be diabolically induced.

Whether or not they have been present in a person's life, they are likely to cease once full union is reached and the Trinity has permanently taken possession of the soul in its very deepest strata, or substance.

Sensation-seeking is natural for most of us, and so it is the visibly extraordinary that impresses people and brings them flocking to see "the saint." The adulation of the stigmatist Padre Pio is a case in point. Undoubtedly he is an extremely holy person who abhors publicity and the sensation-hungry attentions of the pious. But the indisputable evidence that he indeed has the stigmata brings them in flocks, and though many who come do go away humbled and closer to God, many others merely marvel at the extraordinary and then proceed as soon as possible to do the same over the next reported vision of our Lady, the next child publicly in ecstasy, the next "miraculous" healing. They seem oblivious of the fact that sanctity is a hidden, inward quality evincing itself in an ordinary life transformed by extraordinary love of God and neighbor. Whether or not the sensational manifestations are present is irrelevant. If they do occur they cause acute embarrassment to the holy person, who attempts to conceal them.

The church has always shown a healthy skepticism about all such matters, and its official sanctification procedure seeks to establish indisputable evidence of heroic, consistent virtue, especially faith, hope and charity, over a long period. Any unusual phenomena are examined and assessed in relation to this.

Teresa of Avila is perhaps the best known of the ecstatic mystics. She has left detailed records of her experiences, and she also had a great fund of common sense and a deep humility. Her accounts are valuable for their exactness, variety, down-to-earth analogies, and insistence that such graces are never to be sought for themselves, but are gratuitously given for the sake of others and the church at large. Detachment concerning them is always necessary.

The desirable end of the life of prayer is pure contemplation received in faith. The lives of Jesus and Mary reveal how deeply concealed beneath the apparently ordinary the most eminent holiness may be.

In all else, it is necessary to remember that the human recording and interpreting apparatus is faulty, even when the message, or experience, is indeed God-given and genuinely extraordinary. The test of authenticity is the existence of heroic virtue in the recipient's life and whether others are influenced by it to greater love and service of God and neighbor.

Since this book is about a state of union that is nothing less than complete and permanent possession of the soul by God, it is useful to examine some of the personal records of those who have experienced extraordinary mystical phenomena in prayer, and have also been officially stamped "saint" by the church.

Teresa of Avila writes from personal experience about spiritual marriage, or transforming union, in the last section of her treatise on union with God, called *The Interior Castle*. The seventh or last mansion describes the summit of love and fulfillment which she herself did not attain till five years before her death. It was during these last years that she composed *The Interior Castle*.

She had had a vision of a crystal castle filled with light emanating from its innermost part where God himself dwelt in bliss and glory. The nearer she came to this center, the more intense the splendor and beauty. Then, as she watched, entranced, the light vanished. Darkness, foul smells, and vile, predatory creatures invaded the castle from outside its walls and violated it.

She then understood how the light of glory showed God present and reigning in the soul, and its blotting out and violation showed the effects of sin on what was meant to be a palace filled with the blessing and joy of the divine presence.

When, under obedience, she wrote her last book on prayer, she developed the theme. In it she is not laying down general rules and specific states that must be followed and attained by all, but describing as best she can, thinly disguised, what happened to and in her, and how it is between her and God at this last stage of her spiritual journey.

All must pass from darkness into full light if they are to attain the beatific vision, but the way, how, and the time are in God's care

and known only to him. Usually we understand something of what
has happened only after the event when, enlightened by the Spirit,
we look back on our experience, and see the pattern at last. If, on
the contrary, we pass out of this life without having attained any
deep union with God, we have to go through purgatorial read-
justments before we can bear to see his glory face to face. We have
to be cleansed by the living flames of his love before we can give
ourselves to absorption into it in final fulfillment.

Teresa speaks of the light that emanates from the Trinity's indwelling to establish heaven within. What I would call "the prayer
of the innermost center" then occurs in that dwelling place God
himself has shaped, chosen and filled with his grace. This is the
seventh mansion and the soul's own center.

Teresa teaches that in this mansion raptures in which consciousness is lost are past. Visions are now not imaginary but "intellectual," coming through infused knowledge and insight into the
mysteries of the Trinity and especially of their graced presence in
the mystery of hidden love. This greatly heightened prayer of awareness has no visible forms, though Teresa speaks of a "cloud of the
greatest brightness" which, of course, is a direct contrast to the dark
cloud of unknowing that has enveloped the soul during the years
of purgation.

In our spiritual depths that are most impenetrable to any natural manner of entry we have communicated to us with absolute
certainty that the presence of the Three-in-One is an experiential
fact. "They are in the interior of her heart—in the most interior
place of all and in its greatest depths," yet there are no raptures. We
remain alert and able to carry on with ordinary life while this divine
love pours itself out upon others and on our environment, using us
as its channel. We are given a calm certainty that this is not a transitory, but a "forever" grace. God is not just visiting—he has made
his permanent abode with us.

The awareness of Presence and of the degree of penetration is
at times acute, but it fluctuates. However, it is never obliterated.
Even when our attention is distracted from it, we retain a convincing
though obscure sense of its actuality and the companionship it
blesses us with. Our concentration upon God ebbs and flows ac-

cording to his will, not ours, but in spite of the tides, the ocean remains where it is.

Though trials and sufferings persist to a greater or lesser degree, the rock-bottom certainty and comfort of permanent Presence never alters, and so we cannot be overwhelmed by desolation and the dread that God has abandoned us as at times during the deeper passive purgations.

A curious sense of being split in two results. Teresa speaks of "the division between soul and spirit." It is almost as if one part of us is dissociated from the other so that both are functioning separately at different levels. We may be suffering and distressed in "the faculties," but underneath is that substrata of peaceful resting in the surety of the Lord's entrenched and loving support. This never fails us once transforming union is attained. And yet this is not the perfect fulfillment promised us in the next life, but only a foretaste of its essential quality.

Teresa differentiates between the betrothal and the marriage, and John of the Cross does the same. In the first there are times of separation, in the second "the two are united so that they cannot be separated anymore." After all, human marriage is essentially a permanent two-in-one flesh union, and spiritual marriage is similar, but in the spiritual sphere. The authentic stamp of any marriage is its indissolubility. If that is not present, there is no marriage, only a temporary union.

Spiritual marriage is also with the risen Lord who needs no door to come into the soul's secret, deepest center and pronounce his blessing of peace as he did to the apostles. He transfers his resurrection glory to it, and Spirit mingles with spirit in final and full union.

Teresa compares this to rain falling into a river or spring, or a streamlet entering the sea. The waters so permeate each other as to be indistinguishable and inseparable (like the water and wine in the chalice at the eucharist). Similarly light that enters a room through two large windows "enters in different places but it all becomes one."

Centered in Christ, and only in Christ, his Father and his Spirit, we can now affirm with Paul that we do "live" in the truest sense because the life in us is Christ's own resurrection love-life. We are constantly fed by it, drenched in its peace, in a paradoxical state of absolute spiritual poverty and need for God, coupled with absolute fulfillment and possession of all we desire in him. Our self-empty-ing, accomplished through full cooperation with grace, has made a void of inner space like a giant reservoir brimming with living water which now pours out from us for the whole world.

We are servants of all with the Servant of all who came as the Redeemer of all. Our one desire is to be used by him for that mighty work of his. Bound to him in this, we yet share the glorious liberty that is his by right. With the utmost care we refrain "from commit-ting the smallest offense against God, and suffer at how little [we] are able to do and how great is the extent of [our] obligations."

We are conscious that, though all that we give our Bridegroom is only a widow's mite, it is at the same time also the munificence of all God's resources through Christ, whom we now fully possess and who possesses us. As permanent receptacles of this new life, Teresa tells us we are characterized by the following: self-forgetfulness; absence of merit-seeking; complete trust in God; a readiness to die coupled with a contrasting desire to live in order to be able to suffer and work for souls and for God's honor and glory; desirelessness regarding everything but this; a lack of egotism and self-absorption; an over-ruling passion for God's will to be done in and through us, together with a conviction that whatever he wills is beneficial; joy in persecution and a special love for enemies plus a readiness to be deprived ourselves so that they "may be prevented from offending our Lord."

"Our conception of glory," she writes, "is being able in some way to help the Crucified" in his redemptive work.

We have in abundance the grace of holy indifference. Trivial-ities have no power to preoccupy us. We do not fear death, and in our detachment we seek solitude so we can remain uninterruptedly in communion with the Presence within, yet at the same time we have a constant urge to be "busy with something that is to some soul's advantage."

We are constantly led by the Spirit, whose gentle promptings move from deep within upward to the surface of consciousness, where they issue in action always characterized by sacrificial love and perfect obedience to God's will.

There is now no fear of delusion and the certainty that such promptings come from God is serene. From this innermost mansion he reaches out spiritually to make "touches" of love on our soul's very substance. These "prepare the soul to be able to do, with a resolute will, what he has commanded it." Thus we are always obedient, good and profitable servants whose actions bring forth good fruit for the kingdom since they are done in God, for God, and by means of God's power.

The devil has no way of approaching this innermost center where the indwelling is. Everything is so deeply interior that he is powerless to influence it through his only route of the faculties and senses in the outer mansions of the castle. Neither Satan, nor anyone, nor anything can now frighten or disturb us in any significant way (though surface disturbances, with or without Satan's involvement, may recur), for we now possess the strength of Christ in abundance and in it our human weakness is totally absorbed. Peace reigns, for at last our priorities are unyieldingly in place exactly where God wants them to be.

It is as if the Bridegroom was kissing and embracing the soul, making his presence so indelibly experienced that it can and will never be obliterated. We are sealed with his seal forever.

This is what I call "The Prayer of Presence, Penetration and Union" in which a human being is transformed into an aspect of the divine—an earthenware vessel that indeed holds a treasure past telling.

Section IV of the seventh mansion stresses that out of this union of spiritual marriage apostolic works of great importance to Christ's redemptive plan must and do issue (though not necessarily overtly). We are now very especially called to serve Christ's body, for in our "perfect" state we are at last completely docile and so can be used by God exactly in accordance with his will and plans. He gives us the humility to receive his promptings clearly, and the strength to act as they indicate. We are now his weapons against sin, his instruments of salvation, his servants of anyone and everyone, so as to draw them also into his blessed embrace.

Teresa sums it up in a most memorable and convincing passage: "The soul's whole thought will be concentrated upon finding ways to please him and upon showing him how it loves him. This, my daughters, is the aim of prayer: this is the purpose of the spiritual marriage, of which are born good works and good works alone. . . . Do you know when people really become spiritual? It is when they become the slaves of God and are branded with his sign, which is the sign of the Cross, in token that they have given him their freedom. Then he can sell them as slaves to the whole world, as he himself was sold, and if he does this he will be doing them no wrong but showing them no slight favor. . . . His food consists in our bringing him souls, in every possible way, so that they may be saved and may praise him for ever."

With her usual sound common sense, she points out that such self-oblation seldom entails spectacular sacrifices and works obvious to all, but exists in "setting our hand to the work which lies nearest to us, and thus serving our Lord in ways within our power. . . . Apart from praying for people, by which you can do a great deal for them, do not try to help everybody, but limit yourselves to your own companions. Your work will then be all the more effective because you have the greater obligation to do it. . . . By your doing things which you really can do, His Majesty will know that you would like to do many more, and thus he will reward you exactly as if you had won many souls for him. . . . The Lord does not look so much at the magnitude of anything we do as at the love with which we do it."

Through the summary given in this chapter of her thought, it is clear that Teresa knows exactly what it is like to be filled with resurrection love-life, and she also knows exactly what God wants us to do with what he has so bountifully given us.

And that is: Pass it on to others in love and humility.

CONFUSION OF ROLES

I thought I knew something of this place
both from experience and maps.
But now I'm here, I'm overcome with wonder.
There's such an air of spaciousness,
such artistry of light encountering shade,
such balancing of shapes in accurate design,
such originality in form and feature.

My eye delights itself, while I stand here
amazed at such perfection I could not myself
have ever formulated, let alone
brought into being in immaculate right order.

Your gracious ways are past imagining. You
have made me welcome here as to my home.
You told me I belonged here, could stay forever
if I wished, yet if I chose to go
you would not hinder me or countermand my freedom.
Though Master of this palace, you acted as my servant,
knelt and washed my feet, stood there
girded in a towel, humbly asking me
what else I needed to adorn my bliss.

You treat me not as guest, but mistress of the house.
I bow my head in shame.
You do not seem to recognize or take into account
that I am the unprofitable servant,
you the Master and my Lord.

The Resting Prayer

Most of us will not receive the kinds of graces that Teresa and John of the Cross write about, but this does not exclude us from attaining the fullest degree of union with God. This consists not in extraordinary manifestations but in total merging in faith of a human will (i.e. heart) with the divine will.

Jesus said, "I do always the things that please him." To live thus is to live in the third syndrome, resurrection love-life, transforming union, spiritual marriage and the kingdom of heaven within. We always do what pleases God if we never fail to act in accordance with his will, implicit and explicit, at whatever cost to ourselves, and for the sole motive of love. Exalted experiences, though blissful and precious, are only the icing on the cake, as it were.

Reginald Garrigou-Lagrange, O.P. nicely summarizes the fundamental nature of the gifted state of spiritual perfection in his exhaustive study, *Christian Perfection and Contemplation*.

"The supernatural prayer of which St. Teresa speaks, which ought always to unite the soul more closely to God, is sometimes accompanied by ecstasy, by interior words, or even by visions. Yet these things are only accidental and transitory phenomena which pass, while infused contemplation continues. . . . We can easily harmonize four recently proposed opinions as to the nature of the mystical state.

"The first holds that it consists in an infused knowledge of God and of divine things; the second, in an infused love; the third, in a special passivity of the soul more acted upon than acting; and the fourth, in a simple and loving attention to God. The last cannot, in fact, be prolonged without a rather manifest intervention of the gifts [of the Holy Spirit]."

This succinct résumé reaches behind the more unusual manifestations of spiritual union to the deep reality that is permanent. It stresses that the prayer of resting and embrace (and any other kind of prayer characteristic of transforming union, of which I have tried to present a selection in this book) is a special grace from God. The Spirit gives ("infuses") and we receive ("in passivity of soul")—that in a state of resting and abandonment.

Awareness of what is being given is a separate grace. We may, in fact, be having knowledge and love infused into us while we are resting so deeply in the Lord's embrace that we are physically asleep. Our recording apparatus is switched off. Yet, at a later time, what has been given invades our consciousness—like the diamonds and crystals swirled to the surface in the Pool of Tranquillity.

Union can happen, be there and operative, in such a quiet, uneventful, unobtrusive way that all we know is that we are profoundly at peace, that the peace comes from God, and that we know exactly what we have to do right now. The prayer of peace in the depths is obviously allied to the resting prayer, for both have trust and faith as their basis.

Jesus gives a living example of both prayers in Mark 4:35–41. Exhausted from teaching the crowds, he decides to cross over by boat with the disciples to the other side of the lake, away from the demands and proximity of the people. He is so tired that all he wants to do is rest, so he settles himself in the stern and goes to sleep. Mark adds the touching comment, "with his head on a cushion."

A storm blows up so fiercely that the gale makes waves break over the open boat, threatening to swamp and sink it. The disciples are terrified, but Jesus sleeps on unperturbed.

Too exhausted to waken?

Or trusting so perfectly in the Father's care that he knows that no storm will harm them on this journey—no matter what the future holds?

The disciples, lacking such trust, shake him awake, even reproaching him for not caring about their welfare. They confuse his state of resting in God in perfect trust with culpable indifference to their and his own safety. And yet they obviously think he is able to do something to remedy their situation.

As if humoring them, as well as teaching them a lesson about the power of God to save, he speaks to the storm in much the same manner as one would command a savage dog threatening to attack, but of which one has no fear.

"Quiet now! Be calm!"

All the fury dies away in an instant. He now rebukes the disciples for being so frightened and lacking faith. Naturally, they are overcome with awe and confusion at this living parable in which they themselves have played a prominent part.

Jesus was exhausted.

He rested.

When he rested, he rested in God.

When it was necessary to act, he did so in God's power. No peril could shake his faith and no threat could lessen his trust, and so he could sleep in peace through a tempest. The parallels in our own lives are obvious.

At another time he told the people, "Come to me, all you who labor and are over-burdened, and I will give you rest. Shoulder my yoke and learn from me, for I am gentle and humble in heart, and you will find rest for your souls. Yes, my yoke is easy and my burden light" (Mt 11:28–30).

Several important points about this invitation need comment.

Jesus tells us to *come*. We are to make that effort of choosing a purpose and direction by deliberately turning to him in our need. When we experience life as crushing us, he is the one who can and will help, but he does not force himself upon us. It is up to us to respond freely to his offer of help, and then he will give us his own peace, his own ability to rest in God even when the worst threatens.

The yoke he refers to is a double one linking two beasts of burden who together pull the load and share the work. We are reminded of Isaiah's hymn to the suffering servant who bears our sufferings and sorrows, is punished and crushed for our sins, brings us peace through these sufferings and heals our wounds with his own.

In Isaiah Jesus is doing all the work for us. In the New Testament, the fullness of the redemption message, he is inviting us to find meaning, purpose and peace in becoming a beast of burden with him, harnessed into the same yoke. He has come to make us one with him, and he is indicating the means commonly encountered by us all in everyday life—that of willingly shouldering his burden with a work-mate, and so halving it and turning the work into a labor of love.

He accepts his yoke in humility, and because he is at peace with it, it loses its power to crush him. We shall find that the same is true for us if only we respond to his invitation. We need never be alone again in our troubles. We shall even "find rest" in the midst of them through his presence within us sharing them with us.

He promised, "Behold, I am with you all days—even to the end of the world" (Mt 28:20).

The resting prayer is not concerned only with our dark times, but with all aspects of our lives. Whatever our circumstances, Jesus calls us to rest in and with him, certain of his help and strength, his enabling grace. In a sense he himself rested even on the cross, for he made no effort to come down from it, though he knew that, if he chose that course, his Father would send myriads of angels to help him. He accepted his destiny of a cruel death in perfect abandonment to the divine plan for our redemption. He knew that only good could come out of it in the end, for "the prince of the world" and all his works had been overcome by the Son's own perfect resting in God's will (which was, of course, his own will also).

To express it in our own colloquial terms, we need to say to God, "Whatever you do—or let happen to me—it's OK by me"— which is to echo Mary's *fiat* that was her way of resting in the Spirit's embrace to bring about the incarnation and, as a consequence, the salvation of the human race.

For many years in my own life, a symbol for the resting prayer has been the prosaic one of a shabby old chaise lounge with wheels that I have on occasion moved outside under the trees, onto decks and verandas, and from room to room, and window to window. It is adjustable, has springs, is light to manipulate, and with a squab on it is the perfect invitation to put up my feet, to give myself up to contemplation of the beauties and wonders of God and nature, and especially to relax completely in the Lord. To me, physical, mental and spiritual relaxation and bodily resting go together: Jesus had his cushion in the boat—I have had my chaise lounge for well over twenty years!

The resting prayer is an adjunct to abandonment, which is a spiritual state of relaxing completely in God. We lie down in peace in his will as expressed through his divine providence, which is his living embrace in our lives. We rest in him because he is what and who he is, and he dwells within us, always accessible.

Mature faith in the existence and absolute benevolence of God expressed through his personal relationship with each of us engenders trust. How can one help but trust a Being who faith assures us is all-powerful, all-holy and all-loving toward his creation? From that childlike trust, "like a weaned child asleep in its mother's lap," comes the ability to rest in God. We do not need to go anywhere to slip into his embrace, for he is there within, closer than our breath.

Many of us learn and practice physical exercises that facilitate relaxation. The resting prayer needs the discipline of spiritual exercises leading to that perfect inner relaxation indicating full trust in divine providence, God's endless love for us.

Physical relaxation and resting is of course different from the resting prayer, for this occurs in the spiritual dimension. However, a human being is a totality, and the way the body is and feels can have a profound effect on our prayer. Severe physical pain, for example, can so preoccupy us that concentration on anything but it is impossible. At such times our only prayer is an interior act of abandonment, a helpless cry for strength to endure, or the silent will to offer our suffering with that of Jesus in his passion for his redemptive purposes.

There can be nothing cerebral in any of this. It comes from the heart—spontaneous, untutored, little more than a soundless cry of anguish that becomes prayer because it is directed toward God and offered trusting in his help. I have heard a person in such extremity of bodily pain merely muttering over and over, "Oh God—oh God—oh God . . ." I knew that that person's will was open to receive God's will at all times and in whatever way it presented itself, and so his simple cry was uttered in union with the prayers of Jesus in his passion, especially those on the cross, for this was a person of deep faith. The body was torn in anguish, but the inner core, the will, the substance and essence of the soul, rested uncomplainingly in the Father's loving purpose.

During the prayer of resting in God and in the embrace of the Beloved, we deliberately leave behind the cares, problems and preoccupations linked with our daily lives and personal relationships. They are sometimes light, sometimes crushingly heavy baggage we dump on the porch when we come home from a demanding day shopping, or at work, or on a business trip. Leaving it there, we thankfully come into the peace and quiet of the dwelling place where we are able to live consciously in God's presence.

Jesus taught us to go into an inner room to pray and be alone with God.

Having left our everyday luggage on the porch, we deliberately go apart, with empty hands and quiet heart, to be with God and rest in him. We stretch out on our metaphorical chaise lounge, compose ourselves in whatever posture we find most conducive to tranquillity of mind and body, and turn our attention and hearts to God.

We enter the state of holy leisure in which we are more than content simply to gaze at God and love him, as lovers gaze, entranced, into each other's eyes—which is one definition of contemplation.

We "look at him and love him." We need no spate of words—the fewer the better. None at all is best. Jesus has his arms about us and holds us against his heart. We close our eyes and rest there. We stay quietly in passive receptivity, open to his love and his Spirit's messages of infused knowledge, guidance, reassurance, warning and everlasting love.

We rest in God. We are able to because we trust him unwaveringly, and he can do what he likes with us.

It's OK by us. Forever and ever.

Author's Note: Bach provides us with an exquisite musical interpretation of the spiritual state of resting in God in *Cantata No. 82, Ich habe genug,* as sung by Gerard Souzay.

BELOVED (cf. 1 Kgs 19:12)

I believe you—we belong together now.
Inseparably two in one flesh, that is my being.
Experiential facts cannot be denied.

The book says: I am my beloved's
and he is mine. Neatly put. Seven words
one-syllabled—the eighth, the operative,
has three. "Beloved" . . . the invocation echoes
in my deepest caverns. It reverberates
from wall to wall, and distances
too vast to comprehend are filled with whispers
resonating in infinity.

And I recall the still small voice
Elijah heard. After the mighty wind
the earthquake and the pitiless fire
there came a zephyr that caressed
his savaged heart and offered love,
then sent him on ambiguous errands to solve
his problem of wishing to be dead
beneath a furze bush in some anonymous desert.

Likewise your whispering call to love
led me from a desolate landscape
into one vast oasis of security
where you and I go on your errands hand in hand
and I am yours and you are mine
as if two streams had met in confluence
to irrigate this paradise of love
and make an Amazon that sweetens
a whole world's ocean of salt tears.

The Spirit-Filled Prayer

This prayer is especially characteristic of the resurrection love-life state. The Spirit is received by us as one of the Lord's resurrection gifts. It is an essential element of his own transformed state into another dimension of being, and hence of ours.

In his proclamation to the Romans of the good news, Paul stresses that "the spirit of holiness" in Jesus is intimately associated with his resurrection and being plainly revealed as Son of God (cf. Rom 1:3-4). This resurrection power and life is passed on to us through the Spirit, transforming us into aspects of the risen Lord and making us glorious with his own transcendent love-life. He sends the Spirit to us so that we in our turn become "sent" people— witnesses to and proclaimers of the Lord's victory over death and darkness.

The new creation promised at the last supper is fulfilled at Pentecost when the in-rush of resurrection love-life is so potent that those who receive it are changed forever. The tongues of fire (aspects of the living flame of love) convey the outpouring of the Spirit from the Father into the risen Lord and in turn from him into all his followers through the centuries to the present time. Through that pentecostal transfusion we enter the love-joy-fulfillment syndrome, and as a result show forth in life and verbal witness the abundance of divine fullness we have received. Our whole existence now becomes a Spirit-filled prayer from which grace, love and renewal pour out for others, just as they did from the apostles.

They were Amazons of the living waters. Though we in our turn may be only rivulets, we yet genuinely do God's work as people "sent" by the Lord under the influence of the Spirit breathed into us.

This indwelling of the Spirit bestows particular blessings and powers.

One is discernment, especially in relation to sin, judgment and Satan, as Jesus foretold at the last supper. We gain insight into the falsity of the world's standards, and a sensitivity to the presence of Satanic influences. Because this discernment is given by the Spirit of truth it has the stamp of divine authenticity, yet this does not mean we have become incapable of human error, even though our conscience has become a delicate instrument of extreme sensitivity.

It is an inner recording apparatus, indwelt by the Spirit, that intuitively and accurately sees what in our personal life could lead to sin, while it receives insight into semi-conscious, sinful tendencies within both ourselves and others. Such awarenesses lead to an immediate unequivocal "no" to anything that could be an occasion of sin. They are like warning signs before precipices that we come across in broad daylight causing us to change direction immediately.

In order to be saved, human beings must gain insight into the nature of sin and its evil effects both personally and universally. Those in the resurrection love-life state no longer commit any deliberate sin, but they are called to grow daily in divine love and life. For this growth process to continue, their awareness of the extent of the wound of sin within themselves and its involuntary effects in their lives needs to be deepening all the time.

They cannot correct what they do not see or get rid of what seems to them no hindrance. Depth on depth of selfishness and self-will lie concealed in all of us. The Spirit is the depth-charge that reveals what we were unaware of, and at the same time offers us the will and strength to combat it. As the channel of grace, it also gives light to see relationships between Christ's redemptive sufferings and our own inadequacies and rooted sinfulness, so that, for his sake even more than for our own, we deplore and oppose them. Often simple insight is enough to dissolve away such imperfections, for it causes us to relinquish whatever secret attachments that, in the light given by the Spirit of truth, we now realize are harmful.

Every imperfection, even though involuntary, is in some way or other a hindrance to a deepening of resurrection love-life, and needs to be penetrated by grace and so transformed into an aspect of holiness. But first we have to see it for what it is and give our consent to the Sanctifier to act on it.

This divine action is often painless and smooth, for it no longer has to encounter opposition and willfulness in us. We have renounced so much already, usually after fierce battles and much pain. Now it comes spontaneously to say, "Yes, Lord. Certainly, Lord. Anything else, Lord?"

The Spirit-filled prayer has its source in the depths of our being where the indwelling is, for "the real circumcision is in the heart—something not of the letter but of the spirit" (Rom 2:29). The circumcised heart is now possessed by the unadulterated "love of God [that] has been poured into our hearts by the Holy Spirit which has been given us" (Rom 5:6). We want the Spirit to do our praying for us. Only it knows the deep things of God, and we long to live in accordance and union with those depths, even while we realize that their mysteries lie beyond our human understanding. We "groan inwardly" in our longing to immerse ourselves in them and fathom God's will for us, and we have faith that the Spirit can and will give this immersion and understanding, if we wait in humble expectancy for its visitation.

As we wait, it seems to us that we hear its "unutterable groanings" as it intercedes for us, expressing what we ourselves cannot, in a mode beyond our capacity. Mysteriously, these intercessions fulfill our longings and needs, for "God, who knows everything in our hearts, knows perfectly well what [the Spirit] means, and that the pleas of the saints expressed by it are according to the mind of God" (cf. Rom 8:26–27).

The best prayer is often the silent yearning of the dumb heart, and this the Spirit expresses for us as an indelible part of resurrection love-life, now established by its own sanctifying powers within us.

Letting the Spirit pray in and for us presupposes an advanced degree of self-abandonment to divine providence. The Spirit itself deepens this abandonment every time we submit to its "unutterable groanings" and then wait patiently for their mysterious fulfillment, asking for the grace to recognize it for what it is, accept it, and give thanks for it when it does come.

For often, when the Spirit prays in us for us, the results are, to say the least, unexpected!

Because the Spirit has been given the task of instructing us about sin, judgment and the wrongness of the world's attitudes and actions that led to the death of the Savior, it is intensely involved in the continuance of Christ's redemptive work here and now.

The Spirit of the Lord fills the whole world and holds all things in being. If God drew back his Spirit, everything would cease to exist. Only the Spirit knows the deep things of God and the depths in each of us, for it permeates us as well.

It remains a painful mystery that, though the Spirit of love and holiness, the Sanctifier, fills the whole earth, the world remains blighted by sin and evil. Perhaps the explanation is that, if the Spirit was not everywhere, there would be nothing but sin and evil, and our planet would then be hell. Yet, even so, we retain free will and are able to refuse to be led and influenced by the Counselor God has given us.

It is in the people that live on the earth that we find the source of sin and evil, for wickedness has its origin in the human heart. The earth itself is neutral, though we have polluted and despoiled it in a frenzy of exploitative madness.

Sartre observed, "Hell is other people," but heaven is also other people—Spirit-filled people in whom the glory and holiness of God is vibrantly alive and streaming out as a healing, sanctifying force. Before it, sin and evil wither away and Christian hope affirms that it is the Spirit's power that in the end does and will overcome the powers of darkness, and make our hope "boundless" (see Rom 15:13).

Every person in whom resurrection love-life is established and active is as it were a transmitting station for the Spirit's limitless power for good. The divine plan of rescue traced in scripture from creation till the endtime illustrates that the Spirit moves in mysterious ways, yet unerringly toward one end—the salvation of the whole human race. Those in the third syndrome and resurrection love-life are intimately associated with this all-inclusive redemptive plan. The Spirit imbues them with apostolic zeal, and they must be about their Father's work day and night, though not necessarily in dramatic ways.

Each of us is a vessel whose destiny is to be filled with the Spirit. "The life and death of each of us has its influence on others. If we live, we live for the Lord; and if we die, we die for the Lord, so that alive or dead we belong to the Lord" (Rom 14:8). It follows that he can do what he likes with us. And what he wants to do is fill us with his Spirit and then set us to work. At the last supper Jesus explained that he himself had to leave his disciples precisely so that the Advocate, the Spirit of truth, would come to them and empower them to witness to the resurrection and all that it implied. Indeed, this Spirit was already with and in them.

At Pentecost they directly experienced what he had been telling them about, and it changed them forever. They received the promised gift in almost unbearable force, as the Spirit invaded them, baptizing them in its power and grace, and bestowing charismatic gifts to help them in their apostolic task. In an instant they were all raised into the fullness of resurrection love-life and became spiritually inebriated by it.

The Spirit-filled prayer has its origin in the Pentecost event. It is a powerful flow of salvific love directed at that very "world" that is so deeply and tragically at fault. This love uses us in our abandonment as its conduit, pouring out the living waters through us for others by means of prayer, action and hidden oblation. Even while we suffer from the acute awareness of sin's reality, we also live and act in profound faith and hope. Satan and all his works were overcome by Christ in his passion and death. Sharing in his immolation, we also share in his conquest, and know he is using us, through his Spirit, to pass on the healing and blessings he gained for all humankind. He affirmed that he came to save all without exception, and his will cannot be thwarted—only we have to do our part by participating in his redemptive work. Our desire to do so is strengthened and purified by the Spirit's burning love consuming us and the illuminations he gives our minds.

He shows us the redemptive mandala, with Christ on the cross as its center and focal point. Contemplating that tortured figure, we are appalled at what results from sin. He fills our hearts with tenderest love for the stricken Beloved, and our wills with a stern purpose to help him in his labor.

He gives us knowledge and understanding of what sin in our own lives and in the lives of others has brought about—in Jesus, and in past and contemporary society. We glimpse the cumulative effects of the racial sin from Adam and Eve until now, and we are horror-stricken. God incarnate, other people, the whole human race have been most grievously wounded—but instead of provoking defeatism, these insights result in the adamant resolve never to sin deliberately ourselves and also to work and suffer to ameliorate and efface its effects.

Jesus came not to judge and condemn, but to judge and save, and continues to do so through his Spirit of love given us till the endtime. The Holy Spirit puts the whole first and second syndromes in perspective, and shows the true purpose of the third and of resurrection love-life in the divine plan of redemption for us all. We see how the Spirit's work is to sanctify and save.

As Jesus so clearly taught, we are all without exception one in him and part of his incarnation-salvation mystery. Everything each of us does and is affects all the others. We cannot know in this life where those effects will end, or whom we are influencing for good or evil, not just by what we do and say, but by what we *are* in our inner, secret selves.

The Spirit-filled prayer reveals something of these mysteries, and the purpose of the revelation is to inspire us to be and to act. We now possess a very grave sense of responsibility. Each of us is indeed our sisters' and our brothers' keeper. We shall be held to account for what the results of our influence on them finally were. The indwelling Spirit makes us acutely sensitive about these responsibilities.

The Spirit-filled prayer does not usually express itself in any extraordinary way. "Speaking in tongues," for example, was certainly a sign of its action immediately after Pentecost, but such a grace can and more often does occur in an entirely interior and hidden manner. The "tongues" may then be the Spirit's directly infused insights and illuminations about doctrine, plus the power of explaining and illustrating such divine truths so that others are enabled to receive, understand and accept them.

The Spirit works for unity against divisiveness. The "tongues" given us may be a grace of peacemaking, so that we know what to say to promote reconciliation between warring factions and angry people. We may be "honey-tongued" so that our gentle, loving, yet unyielding attitudes and words help others see the enormity of sin, anger, hatred, scorn, and repent and undergo metanoia. Our non-judgmental attitudes, coupled with our ability to reveal where wrong turnings and misunderstandings have occurred, may issue in wise words that are exactly right for this person in this situation. This may occur when we have had no chance to reflect beforehand, for we did not know what or whom we were to encounter.

The Spirit has been given us as counselor and guide. Jesus said not to be afraid if we were brought before hostile authorities when we were innocent, for the Spirit would inspire us what to say. It will do the same in situations where we are led to reveal the truths of the faith to individuals and teach them in a personal, compelling manner that results in their decisive change of heart. The gift of tongues is essentially the ability to make plain to others, in a way they will understand and find acceptable, the facts about their relationships with God and other people that till then they had either repudiated, misunderstood or been ignorant of.

The Spirit is the architect of renewal and the source of the graces that enable it to happen. Renewal means a new start and a radical change of direction and aim. It means enlightenment of heart and strengthening of will to act on what has been revealed. Self-knowledge and self-acceptance lead to repentance and the decision to act. "This is what and how I am. I want to change, to be different. The Spirit will help me." This process may be initiated and carried through in a person without any human intermediary. Or the Spirit-filled prayer in us may take the form of a special discernment issuing in "tongues" that accurately convey to this person exactly what divine Wisdom intends, with resultant metanoia.

If we are graced with the Spirit-filled prayer, we shall be used in such ways as channels for its loving gentleness and precise exposition of truth. There is nothing here that we can pride ourselves on, and much to bring about a deeper humility within us. Paul wrote, "In my speeches and the sermons that I gave, there were none of the arguments that belong to philosophy; only a demonstration of the power of the Spirit" (1 Cor 2:4). "There is a variety of gifts, but always the same Spirit. There are all sorts of service to be done, but always to the same Lord. Working in all sorts of different ways in different people, it is the same God who is working in all of them. The particular way in which the Spirit is given to each person is for a good purpose" (1 Cor 12:4–7).

Perhaps Paul sums it up most succinctly when he writes, "After all, what is Apollos and what is Paul? They are servants who brought the faith to you. Even the different ways in which they brought it were assigned to them by the Lord. I did the planting, Apollos did the watering, but God made things grow. Neither the planter nor the waterer matters: only God, who makes things grow. . . . We are fellow-workers with God" (1 Cor 3:5–9).

Since the Spirit is the expression of God's love, it flows from the Trinity's mutual compenetration, and when the Spirit floods us with its presence, it is as part of the Trinity's indwelling. It follows that the Spirit-filled prayer is the expression of the fathomless, graced love flowing into and out from the human heart possessed by the Trinity. Divine love's deepest expression is in self-giving. It is offered to us to inspire and lead us to the total self-giving that is both holiness and perfect personal fulfillment.

Once immersed in resurrection love-life we are already full of love, yet paradoxically we can become even fuller as the Spirit's power divests us of those flimsy garments of self-protection we did not even realize we still clutched about us. These may be fear of further suffering, self-will over small matters, silly little habits indicating trivial addictions, momentary carelessnesses in speech and action that hurt and distress others, involuntarily taking pride in our apostolic achievements instead of immediately and humbly thanking God for having used us in all our ineptness and unworthiness, gifted though we may well be in various ways . . .

All failures in one way or another of love of God and neighbor are subject to the Spirit's purifying action if only we open ourselves to it. The Spirit-filled prayer shows us where these little failures in the practice of total love are, and helps us to overcome them. Then we can even say of them, "Oh happy faults!" for they have been the route to deeper love and quieter humility and self-acceptance. They have led us further into truth, and our insights have resulted in a more complete oblation of our own will in favor of Spirit-chosen ways of self-expression that benefit others.

Living in the third syndrome does not mean exclusion from the second, and it may even include immersion in the first as a co-proxy with the Savior for those who make no effort to extricate themselves. Love expresses itself in manifold ways, and through the Spirit-filled prayer we are led into the particular modes that God means us individually to use.

We may not feel able to express such artless pride in the results as Paul does at times, yet what he writes to the Romans does have its application to us too.

"I think I have some reason to be proud of what I, in union with Christ Jesus, have been able to do for God. What I am presuming to speak of, of course, is only what Christ himself has done to win the allegiance of the pagans, using what I have said and done by the power of signs and wonders, by the power of the Holy Spirit. . . . This is only what scripture has predicted, and it is all part of the way the eternal God wants things to be. He alone is wisdom. Give glory therefore to him through Jesus Christ forever and ever. Amen" (Rom 15:17–19; 16:26–27).

LANGUAGES

Why must you always speak to me
in Aramaic? Even at 2 a.m.
you're at it! Such a babble
at such an hour! Who could interpret it?
I'm no linguist. Here I am
in urgent need of guidance, hammering
importunately on your door according to
your own instructions, only to encounter
this arcanum in staccato clicks and clacks,
an indecipherable secret code of stipulations
that I cannot understand.

You said to do your will. How can I
if you won't make plain to me its content?
If you won't be specific and tell me what to do?

A lapse into vernacular startles me:
"Nothing," in audible, terse English.
Curt commands require brief responses.
"Thank you!"
                    Then I boil over . . .

Have you forgotten how all this time,
these months and years, yes—years—
that is precisely what I've had to do—
nothing? A prisoner in a cell
of solitary confinement does just that.
I want some action now. I'm worn
to a fine edge of near-despair
after so much unadulterated waiting
for so intolerably long!

What's that you say? Vernacular again?
This one has to be important!
Yes, I'm listening . . . "Patience is a virtue."
All right . . . I get the message . . . I'm sitting here
quite still. I'm calm
                    and quiet
                                        at last.

Speak.

This time you don't use words at all
but plunge into my heart your shaft
of silent revelation. Now I understand
beyond all human language . . . I must sit
and go on sitting . . . composedly . . . right here . . .
and stop my murmuring and fussing so you
can work unhindered out of sight.

There your mystery of love and fond erasure
will atomize my prison door and set me free
to see and understand your ways so I
can float emancipated in nothing but your will.

I capitulate. You win. (You always do.)
Speak to me in Aramaic if you wish.
                              You laugh!
I like that mighty crash of universal mirth.

The Stream of Consciousness

Freud made plain both the existence and the importance of the human stream of consciousness, including its fantasies. We ignore it and its preoccupations at our peril, yet once we have given our hearts and lives to God, in another sense it becomes unimportant. It ceaselessly goes on and on, and will do so till we die. We cannot stop it, but we do not need to identify with it. It operates as a kind of rubbish disposal unit, bearing along fallen leaves that bob on its surface, odds and ends dropped or thrown into it, debris washed off its banks and surroundings in some recent or long-past deluge or deposited in it through a storm-water drain. If it is a free-flowing, deep stream, it deals with all this adequately enough and we need take little notice. During our daily lives we are usually either standing on the bank absentmindedly watching the waters, or are immersed in and floating along unheedingly in the current. At other, more aware times, we may feel the need to struggle purposefully against that current but be unable to oppose it.

In the watching and floating states, as long as we have reached a certain level of detachment so that our will is choosing to identify with God's will rather than idly flow with the stream, saying a careless OK to its contents, our prayer continues. It is arid and distracted, but the distractions are irrelevant, since the seat of prayer is in the will, or heart.

This aridity and distraction is dispelled when and if we receive graces of contemplative prayer. These are bestowed by the Spirit when and how it sees fit. We cannot manufacture them for ourselves, but we can predispose ourselves to receive them by practicing abandonment, detachment, love and perseverance in whatever form of prayer helps us stay close to God. We can also help ourselves by cultivating awareness and deliberate choice of approval or disapproval of what is going on in that stream within us. Once we set to work to do this, we are likely to receive some rather unpleasant surprises.

One of these is the discovery that at certain times the debris in our stream is negative to the point of being noisome and reprehensible. Even in the state of resurrection love-life, which is what we are concerned with in this book, such discoveries are possible. In the earlier stages of our journey our stream was cleared of much of its pollution through our own steady practice of virtue, the graces infused into us, and the passive purgations. Now may come a time when the Spirit decides there is more work to be done, more self-discoveries to be made and a few shock treatments still to be administered.

We have probably already learned that a business-like checking up now and then of what our stream is up to can help our examination of conscience by indicating areas of our interior (and exterior) life that need our active attention. Even in resurrection love-life there may be debris in our stream that is an active agent in serious pollution, but until now we have not consciously realized this, though half-consciously we may have become aware that there was work that needed doing.

It is useful to begin by examining the nature of what hinders our prayer recollection, what is the content of our daydreams (should we still be subject to them, which is unlikely), what it is churning round in our mind and stopping us from going to sleep, and what comes immediately into our thoughts and stays there obsessively and disturbingly should we waken in the night.

If, for example, we discover that worries about money persist in eddying round in our stream and even choking up its flow, we may safely conclude that we lack trust in our Abba, who knows what we need even before we ask for it. The more obsessive the worrying thoughts, even though we may be barely conscious of them, the greater the indication that we need to work harder at the "lilies of the field" approach to life. It is true that our Abba expects us to do whatever is practical within our power to help ourselves before we throw our problems at him. But when we have tried our hardest and end up in an impasse, then is the time for the real test of trust and abandonment to be applied.

One way of doing this is by resolutely opposing worrying thoughts with repetitive affirmations of positive trust in God's power to help and his unfailingly loving will to do so. If we tend to be obsessive, this may be very difficult to do, and our efforts may have to attain the heroic level before we can really let go and let God. Such obsession is not a deliberate fault, even though we may feel much at fault—it is an affliction. And all afflictions and their attendant sufferings can be turned to glorious gain by uniting them with Jesus' afflictions in his passion.

This is what the Spirit is now calling us to do at a depth we could not do before because we did not realize what was going on in our stream of consciousness. In order to continue our examination more effectively, we need to detach part of ourselves and objectify it as Impartial Observer. Observer's role is not to judge, but to watch, note and report to Conscience, who then does the judging and communicates its decision to Will. It is Will who has to decide, "What I have been letting happen in my stream is destructive to trust . . . charity . . . patience . . . hope . . . humility—or whatever else—and I am going to put a stop to it. Every time I catch this particular form of debris polluting my stream, I'm going to fish it out and throw it away. I'm going to disidentify with it. I'm going to stop stamping it 'IMPORTANT.' "

Accomplishing what Will decides may take a long time and much hard work, but the end results will be well worth the effort.

As this book emphasizes, highly graced spiritual states and various kinds of prayers of union do not just fall out of trees upon the refractory and unregenerate. Almost invariably, they come only after stern, dangerous, prolonged interior warfare, and as a result of battles won by means of all our own powers and every grace the Spirit bestows.

When we were graced into resurrection love-life, we realized that we were not put there to rest but to work. Part of this work is cooperating in the continuing purifications that must and will continue till death. The accompanying struggles and sufferings are also meant to be redemptive and so for the sake of our neighbor. We have been "brought back to true life with Christ, and must look for the things that are in heaven, where Christ is, sitting at God's right hand." Now our thoughts are to be "on heavenly things, not on the things that are on the earth, because [we] have died, and now the life [we] have is hidden with Christ in God. But when Christ is revealed, and he is [our] life, [we] too will be revealed in all [our] glory with him" (see Col 3:1-4).

When this fundamental change occurred in us, our conscious wills became captive in God's will. Now the Spirit is leading us into a fuller union with that divine will right down in the subconscious and unwilled area of our non-material being.

Another problem area we are likely to encounter here is that of "unfinished business," which is a difficult, painful one to resolve. It is an inability to step entirely clear of the past. Though we have renounced so much, and accepted so many deprivations, humiliations and defeats in a spirit of abandonment to divine providence and as part of our personal cross, we cannot let go of this obsessive need to recall, relive and be involved with the past. We may need help from someone professionally qualified to guide us through a healing-of-memories process. However, at this stage in our spiritual journey, we can certainly accomplish much through openness to the Spirit's guidance and humble acceptance of what it, often working through Observer, reveals to us. Grace will act deeply if we let it, and we have proved through experience that it can accomplish miracles. We begin to pray earnestly and persistently for it, and we set our Observer to work.

It is rather as if part of our stream had flowed into a bayou or basin at one part of the bank. Here the water begins to eddy, sometimes sluggishly, at others rapidly, in a whirlpool. The debris on and under the surface whirls rhythmically too, its motion automatic and persistent. As we watch it we become almost mesmerized. Observer takes care to point this out to us, and we find the undeniable fact depressing and humiliating.

At times it seems as if we ourselves are immersed in this whirlpool, revolving endlessly round and round in the same pattern, among a medley of odds and ends, many of which we would not care to own in public. (But Observer is always non-judgmental, never emotionally involved.)

There is nothing at all here that we could possibly congratulate ourselves on. We are, against our will, captive in an hypnotic, humiliating, boring, distressing and inescapable situation—a temptation to identify with and consent to the unrealities of memory and imagination.

These consist of situations that were traumatic, in that they often happened without warning. We compulsively relive the events surrounding them, adorning them with imaginary embellishments designed to present them in a more favorable light, and especially to exculpate ourselves.

We may be unable to forget, or let go, the shattering grief to do with the death—perhaps sudden and appalling as in a car accident— of a loved one, or the painful breakup of a very significant personal relationship that had seemed inviolable to misunderstanding and recrimination, and yet has fallen victim to both. Or it may have been public scorn, vilification and rejection regarding a matter over which we were completely innocent.

There are all kinds of variations in human situations that can lead to emotional shocks of such intensity and pain that they cause recurring psychic earthquake aftershocks for years. We can get locked into these and become permanently sad and compelled to go over and over what happened, reimmerse ourselves emotionally in what we felt, nurse our present grief and sense of the irreparable, get buried in the rubble that earthquake spewed up.

Of course Satan capitalizes on this if we permit it. At an earlier stage we may not have realized the danger, but now we are experienced enough in his tactics to be on our guard.

And so, though something masochistic in us wants to keep that whirlpool going round and round while we give our consent to being part of it, we continue to struggle to stay free and Observer helps us with detachment. In spite of temptations to do so, and weariness with the treadmill thoughts, feelings and recalls, we refuse to encourage them with our will. Observer shows us how compulsively we cling to those painful memories, relive all the unfinished business and tidy it up in fantasy and imagination, while lingering pride itches to indulge in self-justifications and recriminations.

We know that such preoccupations are both harmful and sinful. They are also extremely painful. We long and pray and work to be rid of everything to do with them even while, in spite of ourselves, we are unable to let them go. They have become like a bad stammer—an affliction.

Because our deep will remains faithful, grace comes to our help. The Spirit (plus Observer) gives insight. We see that the Sanctifier is causing these upheavals and whirlpools to throw up to our mind's surface material that we must become fully aware of, both as to its content and its harmful effect upon our peace of mind and soul and the further development of a number of important virtues. Above all, we must be led to see how this inner process is a form of self-absorption instead of God-absorption, how tainted it is with self-love and self-will (in spite of all our efforts). We have to face facts honestly, humbly and detachedly.

Some of what we find is likely to be among these realities: All this is part of me. This is what I am like. These are the things I said and did or would like to say and do. This is my reconstruction of the past as I would prefer it to be so as to save face, and restore to me what I am not prepared to relinquish when God indicates it is best for me to be without it. This is the rebel within me saying it will not serve by being abandoned to his will. This is my pride refusing to forgive from the depths of my heart, to be truly humble under misjudgments, to admit defeat and bow before God's might.

This is the dark side of me I would rather not acknowledge and which I try to whitewash in my imagination and dreams, not to mention my endless rationalizations. This is my shadow self and I have been refusing to incorporate it into my conscious self and accept reality, while I rely on grace for the help I must have to do and be better.

Through helping us increase in self-awareness, the Spirit is warning us of the dangers of backsliding into self-preoccupation instead of concentrating on the sacrament of the present moment.

In the past, God let all these things happen while lovingly willing in perfect wisdom only the best ultimate good for both us and our loved ones. If we refuse to become immersed in negativity, we can discover the good fruits he has brought out of what seemed catastrophe. Those good fruits, that victory out of distress, are proof that he is to be trusted. Therefore, in peaceful, untroubled abandonment, our present spiritual task is to place that whole past in his care, certain that the end results of it all cannot be anything but a deeper peace and release for ourselves and others, providing we leave the Spirit free to work.

We do not need to busy our memory and imagination tying up loose ends, making coherent, neat patterns out of what ended in a painful muddle, constructing clever conversations to prove our own guiltlessness, fretting because we cannot now tell a dead or estranged beloved how sorry we are, or express our love in any way . . .

We need to let the contents of that inner whirlpool go free into the full flow of our stream of consciousness. We need to, and must, let it all go so that it is borne away and finally deposited in the ocean of divine love. God will take care of it all for us. Our whole will, conscious and unconscious, must be unified into choosing such renunciation. It is time to stop looking back like Lot's wife, and start really working on living in the eternal now.

A minor miracle of grace is needed, but we have now opened ourselves to receive it, where before we were blind to both its necessity and our own helplessness in the grip of an insidious, persistent, interior temptation against a variety of virtues—trust, humility, charity, faith, hope, perseverance, abandonment, cheerfulness, joy . . . and plenty of others.

The rubbish got rid of, God now begins to infuse into our depths an even more complete peace and freedom in the Spirit. We walk the world more fully in the presence of the risen Christ. Sometimes we experience grace as sinking in from the surface like rain from the high heavens, at others as welling up from subterranean depths as does the artesian water into the Pool of Tranquillity. It brings healing—of memories ("old, unhappy, far-off things, and battles long ago"), of wounds deep or superficial, ancient and going back to the womb, or recent and inescapable as yesterday.

We experience liberation at a very deep level. "Glory be to him whose power, working in us, can do infinitely more than we can ask or imagine" (Eph 3:20). It is as if all evil powers have been dispelled or nullified, all aspects of our being, down into the depths of the subconscious, have been blessed and pronounced good by an all-loving Father who, looking upon what he has made, glorifies it with his own glory.

Our stream of consciousness has become a constant prayer of abandonment imbued with the living waters.

THE KISS OF PEACE

Eve,
I have to live with you.
There's no escape for either of us.
And you're so restless. Couldn't you,
please, cultivate repose?
Be still now and then? Stop
your irritating chatter? Reduce the volume
of those compulsive playbacks of your scripts?

Eve,
we could be quite happy living together
if only you would leave me in my hard-won peace,
if only you'd stop pestering and provoking me.
When do you ever sleep?
When does your fretful pacing cease?
When, my sister, my twin of destiny,
have you ever given up manipulating me?

Eve,
it's not that I want to get rid of you.
You and I need each other—but I long
for truce and harmony between us. Not
this perpetual tug of war—spit, scratch,
accuse, recriminate—all those
tattered resolutions on my part, snarls on yours.
I want a truce, Eve. I want the kiss of peace.

TRANSFORMATION

Live at peace with the wound.
There is no need to finger it. Now
you can leave it be. The blood and water fructify
the blasted landscape. Among the rocks,
in crevices and hollows, on blank hillsides
the miracle of green will soon appear.

Once it was lava seething
from the wound's wide mouth.
Fire, molten rock, rivers of death,
fountains of glittering detritus
flung high into the burning night,
the innermost core's concealed despairs,
cathartic discharge of encumbrances—
the entirety cast to the surface and laid bare.

Now all is tranquil. Cleansing streams
pour from the wound's wide throat.
The sacramental blood and water
transform, heal and bless. The pain is over.
Hosannas fill the sun-drenched air.

Doing Nothing in Stillness

John of the Cross equates this prayer with pure contemplation, the "doing nothing" indicating that we no longer work mentally in meditation by reasonings, images and forms. By contrast, our prayer is normally formless, imageless, wordless and uncontrived. To a large degree it consists of a simple resting in God, or self-abandonment to divine providence, to use the traditional terms, or my own term, floating in endless love. The state is one of waiting patiently for God's visitation, of gazing at him in silent love.

This prayer could equally as well be called "The Stillness Prayer." It places us back where this book began—at the Pool of Tranquillity. Such stillness does not mean the cessation of physical activity in favor of endless navel-gazing, though periods of bodily quiet in order to concentrate on the Presence within are necessary. The stillness is centered in the composed and dedicated will that we feed by deliberately going apart to be alone with God.

When, as lovers of God, we do this, we are never alone with him in the sense of selfish isolation, for we take numberless other human beings with us in our heart to hold them up for the divine blessing. Those who have a vocation to the fullness of physical solitude and silence become hermits or members of enclosed contemplative orders. The prime work given them by the Spirit, their special charism, is that of concentrated prayer and secret but total self-offering in which their lives are "poured away as a libation" (2 Tim 4:6) for anyone and everyone.

This is a very special and spiritually powerful vocation given to few. Critics condemn such a way of life as "useless" because its practitioners are "doing nothing" and there are no observable beneficial results either for themselves or for others. In reality, that "nothing" is the "everything" of unconditional self-offering for others through lifelong, voluntary imprisonment, or withdrawal, in order to be available in a total way to God for those others. The vocation has meaning and purpose for those to whom it is given, but none for the majority who have no faith in the intense power for good for the world of concentrated being-with-God in prayer.

Most of us do not receive this vocation, and even if we are called to a religious order, it will probably be one concerned more with the corporal works of mercy than with the spiritual works of mercy. This is even more so for the majority of believers whose vocation is clearly to live and work in society, actively involved with other people and in local, national and international affairs.

All these apostolates and vocations are blessed by God if they are what we are called to by him and we carry them out in a spirit of prayer. All are necessary for the building up of the body of Christ. All vocations, all gifts and graces are given for the common good, says Paul in 1 Corinthians 14:26. In the same letter he writes: "There is a variety of gifts but always the same Spirit. There are all sorts of service to be done but always to the same Lord. Working in all sorts of different ways in different people, it is the same God who is working in all of them" (1 Cor 12:4-6).

When we go to the Pool of Tranquillity to drink, to gaze into its depths, to glimpse mirrored there the Lord's countenance and mysteriously glimmering through it, our own, we take with us the human race as well as certain specific, personally known people. We drink the holy waters to revive and heal them as well as ourselves. When we see the Lord's reflection, it is not only our own that is merged with it, but that of all those we love, pray and make sacrifices for. Beyond them, we see in the Spirit, and compassionately serve and reach out to in love, untold numbers whose plight we have become aware of perhaps only on TV or from what we read.

Though we cannot personally make contact with them, we can do so spiritually in the dynamic dimension of prayer. In one sense we can "do nothing" for them. In another sense that "nothing" can be "everything" because we are open channels, scoured out in the night of the spirit to receive divine love, and it is coursing freely through us for whomever God chooses.

Most of us will be directly involved, through the activities and contacts of our daily lives, with specific circles of people—family members, spouses, work and leisure companions, intimate friends, casual acquaintances and associates, those we help and those who help us. The circle may be narrow or very wide—shallow and ephemeral with mere acquaintances, or with our much-loved intimates dynamic and of the utmost importance to us.

Whatever their nature, every one of them can be a way into God for all participants. If we ourselves are absorbed in the prayer of stillness and doing nothing in that secret spiritual level far below (or above) the surface hubbub and activity of our lives, Something, or rather Someone, inevitably passes from us into others, and from them into us. This interchange is almost impossible to define or locate, yet it can be compelling and vivid. Perhaps the endless circulatory, pulsing movement of blood through the human body, unseen, not even thought of, yet essential for life, is the best analogy. Humanity is Christ's body, for he identifies himself unequivocally with, and came to save, all of us. The baptized are a vital, specifically designated part of this body chosen to be the vehicles of the good news to all the others. Among the baptized, the unconditionally committed and prayer-permeated are an exceedingly important part. However, the life-blood of Christ's saving love does not differentiate, but constantly circulates around the whole body through his extended incarnation.

We are meant to see and find him in every other human being, and to serve that person as we would Jesus incarnate. He himself is the Something or Someone mysteriously being communicated in our human interactions, for he assured us that whatever we did to others, whether important or not to us or to anyone else, we did to him. Alas for us who think we are such "good Christians."

This book is directed principally to those in whose lives prayer of a contemplative nature is practiced regularly and is regarded—together with the sacraments—as the lifeline for the transmission to others of the resurrection love-life Jesus gives us. The level of awareness in both transmitter and recipient of what is happening will vary greatly. There are people who radiate and put into practice such a dynamic, selfless kindness to all and sundry that Christ shines through them and their lives. They may not be committed to Christianity in any formal way, but they are certainly Christed. They often do mighty works of loving care in a practical sense that witness to the glory of the grace they have received, irrespective of any or no dogmatic commitments.

Such pure love can flow only through a will integrated with God's, its own selfish desires and drives quelled by the stillness of the Spirit deep within, and by the basic drive to "do nothing" but love. In this instance the "do nothing" is expressing itself in obvious works of mercy—rescuing street kids or battered children; caring for the destitute and homeless; running hospices for the incurably ill and dying; treating AIDS victims like cherished human beings instead of pariahs; working in refugee camps; fostering problem children; befriending prisoners and the mentally and/or emotionally ill . . .

The outlets are endless that the do-nothing-but-love people use to express that love. In the stillness of their God-possessed and God-orientated hearts, Christ is incarnated again and expressing himself through them, though they may not even be aware that it is he compelling them to action. If asked, they will say, "I just love people."

If we consider those who, though not in an enclosed, contemplative order, yet are vibrant with resurrection love-life, we find many gradations between exceedingly active lives and those that are much less obviously involved with people in any overt way. These latter spend much of their time in prayer, or prayerful occupations that leave their minds free to dwell on God and let his love flow through them for others.

Their vocation tends more to the spiritual works of mercy. They are likely to be to some degree "hidden away with Christ in God" in the sense that silence and solitude, as far as their life circumstances and duties permit, are essential to them for their body-mind-spirit entity to function smoothly and effectively. Illness, handicaps or age may give them no alternative but to be "shut-ins," yet they are anything but spiritually enclosed. Their hearts are wide open for others.

In one way or another they will have developed a technique for attaining inner stillness and for apparently "doing nothing" in prayer. John of the Cross in *Living Flame* explains that this is the state of "detachment and emptiness of sense and spirit" brought about by the disciplines and purgations of the active and passive nights (III, 47-66). The time for structured meditation is past, and the time for receptivity in stillness by the Pool of Tranquillity has come. What is now required of us is waiting in patience and hope to receive the Spirit's infused gifts, for God "will build supernaturally in each soul the building that he desires" (47). He will surely "enter the soul that is empty and fill it with divine blessings." The doing nothing and the stillness are proofs that a state of spiritual poverty has been reached, and the fulfillment that Jesus promised is here. "Blessed are the poor in spirit; theirs is the kingdom of heaven" (Mt 5:3).

To be truly poor is to want and have (spiritually speaking) nothing but God and his will. It is then that the Trinity find no hindrance to entering and making their home in us.

John of the Cross is most severely critical of those directors who do not understand and have no personal experience of what is happening in the prayer of those contemplatives they seek to guide. Such directors say "The soul is making no progress, for it is doing nothing!" (47) and try to force it back into discursive prayer, calling its "doing nothing" in "stillness" a delusion. John stresses that union with God comes through faith and belief, not through the understanding and reason, for no matter how clever we are and however profound our notions of God, we shall never be able to "understand" him and his ways, or forge union with him through the reasoning intellect.

The doing nothing prayer is typical of the apophatic state. Having received the grace of being still and knowing God in infused faith and love, we have learned from experience that he is indescribable, incomprehensible and unattainable except through immersion in the cloud of unknowing. This immersion cannot be accomplished by our own will, though we can prepare ourselves for it by living for God and neighbor with an undivided heart.

It is natural for us to think of and describe God and our relationship with him in terms of our human life and attributes—to be anthropomorphic. Enlightenments do come through such analogies. They were used by Jesus himself in his parables and teachings. However, when the grace of direct interior experience of the in-dwelling is given us, we learn that God indeed "dwells in inaccessible light" (1 Tim 6:16). We are too time- and earth-bound to understand his otherness. All we can do is stay still and silent in his presence, gazing at and loving him, for only then do we "know" him with the heart, though not with the cleverness of the human intellect, nor through reasoned meditations that give us the comfortable assurance that we have prayed well.

We have to "walk in faith, believing and not understanding" (48), and then God infuses himself into our inner being. Paradoxically, God by "communicating to the soul light and love together . . . produces in us loving, supernatural knowledge . . . which is confused and obscure to the understanding" and seems like "a ray of darkness" to it (49).

This imageless, formless, loving awareness of God's presence is contemplation. It is the stillness of doing nothing but receive in passive, loving openness and abandonment what God is giving. Now it is he who acts in and through us, and his Spirit who guides and enlightens us in a prayer of delicate communication and of secret loving. We do not and could not "make" this prayer as we "make" a meditation. The Spirit infuses it into us, while we wait in silent peace and readiness.

If we persevere in this apophatic emptiness and darkness, we are (without realizing it, though an experienced director will) "going forward, even though [we] have no particular perception" of what is happening. Though we do not feel it in the emotions, we are "soaring upward to God above all things, since [we] take no pleasure in anything" (cf. The Floating Prayer). In this state of paradoxical emptiness that is fullness "nothing gives [us] so much pleasure as that solitary quiet" (51). It is a condition of "holy rest [in a] quiet and peaceful state of recollection" (53). It should never be interfered with or condemned by our telling ourselves, or anyone else chiding us, "You are wasting your time. You must make an effort and pray as you used to with proper discursive techniques, and not imagine you are communicating with God when you are just being lazy!"

John of the Cross severely chides such ignorant critics. "Such persons have no knowledge of what is spirituality. They offer a great insult and great irreverence to God by laying their coarse hands where God is working" (54).

We ourselves, when feeling arid and empty, can easily think that our immersion in such apparent non-prayer, which some intuition tells us is in fact very profound prayer, is a waste of time and we should return deliberately to our former ways, for then at least we could be certain that we were "doing something." If so, we would place a barrier of self-will and wrong choice between ourselves and the peaceful "feeding wholly upon God himself" in that solitude he has placed us in, or placed in us, and through which "he absorbs [us] in himself through these solitary and spiritual unctions" (63).

Here John uses a metaphor that links up with mine of the Pool of Tranquillity. He writes that the devil capitalizes on our taking the wrong direction—i.e. backward—in prayer. He drags us forth like fish "from the depths of the pure waters of the spirit, where [we] had no support or foothold, but [were] engulfed and immersed in God." He flips us onto the bank of the intellect where all we can do is walk laboriously on our own feet "instead of floating in the waters of Siloe, that go with silence, bathed in the unctions of God" (64).

It is a tragedy to have an ignorant, clumsy director during the transition stage from meditation to contemplation, and it is a great blessing to have a wise, informed, sensitively aware guide. Alas, there are few of them, but if we are without one, and trust God, our Abba, in childlike simplicity, his Spirit will lead us safely through any traps and temptations.

Contemplation is *work,* being a state of advanced love-union with God, in which our contribution is vigilant, assiduous practice of the virtues in life outside specific prayer times, and patient waiting upon God in stillness and love during the "doing nothing" periods.

In *Spiritual Canticle,* after recalling the story of Martha and Mary, John stresses how Mary, so highly commended by Jesus, was apparently "doing nothing" and simply "resting in the Lord." Yet the hidden truth was that she was loving him ardently, and "there is no better or more necessary work than love." And he adds categorically that "a very little of this pure love is more precious, in the sight of God and the soul, and of greater profit to the Church, even though the soul appear to be doing nothing, than all these other works together. . . . After all, it was to reach this goal of love that we were created" (*Spiritual Canticle* XXVIII, 1, 2, 3).

The operational word is *pure,* that is, cleansed of all self-will and self-seeking. Whether the love is pure in this way is indicated by the quality of life and love in our relationships with others and our degree of readiness to sacrifice ourselves for them and for God. There is room for self-delusion here, and help is at times needed to know ourselves better and correct where we are falling short so that our prayer of doing nothing in stillness is indeed the fruit of genuine love and the means of growing abundantly in that love.

Then we can joyfully praise and thank God for the grace of what John calls "holy leisure" (*Spiritual Canticle* XXVIII, 4).

Doing nothing in this way does not mean that we shall not be pestered by distractions or on occasion afflicted by aridity, but the distractions somehow remain on the surface, and the aridity is no longer crucifying, but, in a strange way, consoling.

The prayer of doing nothing in stillness is a special grace given us by God for a special purpose—that we shall love and serve him and our neighbor with an even purer heart and greater self-bestowal. It is also a foretaste of heaven where we shall "know" the Trinity face to face, and love heart to heart, without any flaws at all.

EMPTY HANDS

They hold so much, those empty hands.
I see them, palms cupped upward,
resting on her thighs.
Her feet repose composedly together.
Her eyes are closed, face smoothed
as if in sleep or death. Her tranquil fingers
are like flowers widespread to rain's libation.

It is a habit she has cultivated
to sit so quietly with empty hands
waiting. A stone Buddha is not more composed.
Her eyelids do not even quiver. She is lifted up
above all storms. She floats in endless love.

And drifting in and out between
her fingers that clasp nothing
the Spirit's tenuous blessings ebb and flow,
delicately anointing each holy moment
with the balm of limpid peace.

The Living Waters Prayer

Whereas the stream of consciousness is often polluted, the living waters never are.

In this prayer the Pool of Tranquillity is brimming over freely and irrigating all the land about it. Sometimes it flows with urgency in a torrent, but often it moves gently in half-hidden rivulets finding their way secretly among the boulders and undergrowth. Whatever the manner of their movement, the waters cause new growth and revive wilting plants wherever they go.

Their source is deep in the concealed rock strata where the pure artesian wells are trapped, but now find their way into the base of the pool and are driven upward by the underground pressures to overflow forcefully.

The rock strata represent the ground of our being, the secret depths which the Trinity has finally permeated through the passive purgations. The ultimate source of eternal life is now present and active in us, and has infused into our upper level state (our individual spirituality that operates consciously) its grace and presence to deify us. The upwellings occur when grace is so active and predominant in our lives that the Spirit takes charge, diffusing blessedness both into us and through us into our environment. This is a special grace given or not as God chooses. We have no control over its advent or its cessation.

Our role is to stay receptive and passive, ready to act on the

Spirit's initiative when it impels us to express outwardly through its traditional gifts and fruits the loving kindness given us.

The living waters prayer is sublime and recurs as an essential attribute of transforming union. It is, as it were, the lubrication for resurrection love-life. It is part of "the new heaven and new earth" of the Jerusalem on high, and is "the rightful inheritance of the one who proves victorious" (Rev 21:1, 7), and who knows that victory comes not in his own strength but in that of the risen, conquering Lord. "The river of life" flows from the crucified Savior's side, and from the "throne of God and of the Lamb, crystal-clear, down the middle of the street" of John's visionary, heavenly city of love and glory (Rev 22:1–2). Wherever it goes, abundant life is evident and it never ceases renewing itself in us, whether in time or in eternity. Whenever we thirst, we are to come to it and drink freely.

Once our love-life is that of the risen and glorified Lord, the prayer of the living waters permeates our whole existence, pouring grace into and through us. When troubled or in need, we recall its presence and drink in trust and faith, so that our strength and peace are restored. Taking up the bed of our fears, we then walk steadily and with courage into whatever God is requiring of us. Aware of already living spiritually in the resurrection state, we know that our Redeemer lives, that we live with his life in us, and that nothing and no one can now separate us from him and his love. "Neither death nor life, no angel, no prince, nothing that exists, nothing still to come, not any power, or height or depth, nor any created thing, can ever come between us and the love of God made visible in Christ Jesus our Lord" (Rom 8:38–39).

The living waters prayer has this quality of finality and rocklike security. It is as if we drank it at the breast of God as freely as a babe carried or held against its mother's breast, its mouth fastened on the nipple. It drinks its fill, dozes, with eyes closed, suckles again for a few seconds, dozes, suckles, sleeps. Its bliss is so quiet and sure that the mother herself partakes of it. She gazes at her babe, knowing it is "filled with all the fullness" she has to offer—replete physically and emotionally, relaxed in trust in her arms that hold it linked to the source of its life and strength and growth.

Nursing mothers, of whom I have been one, will know exactly

what I mean. In the living waters prayer, God is our mother and we are the suckling babe. Adult and living alongside the Pool of Tranquillity, we drink of the waters he offers in the form of spiritual blessings intimately associated with the presence and action of the Spirit in our lives and prayer. We have been baptized in the Spirit, and the intercommunion is deep and penetrating. Now it fructifies all we are and do, initiating and sustaining the resurrection love-life within us and causing it to issue and find expression through the living waters prayer.

Jesus promised, "The water that I shall give will turn into a spring inside him, welling up to eternal life" (Jn 4:14).

And: " 'If anyone is thirsty, let him come to me! Let the man come and drink who believes in me! As scripture says: From his breast shall flow fountains of living water.' He was speaking of the Spirit whom those who believed in him were to receive" (Jn 7: 38–39).

We came. We believed. We drank. And we have become conduits for those living waters Jesus promised. The final effects on our personal lives, and, by extension, on the lives of others, we will know accurately only in the heavenly face-to-face encounter. Floating in the waters, and washed clean, the presence of the glorified Christ shines through us while his Spirit manifests itself in all aspects of our existence. All we do and are is borne along in the Amazon of grace which, as part of that apocalyptic river from the throne, spreads about it divine live for the life of the world. It laves us in the mystery of the indwelling and our communion in it with one another.

To lower ourselves into its flux is to contact the source of all life and be renewed at all levels of being.

St. Teresa equates the drinking of the living waters with "perfect contemplation," and explains: "God does not allow us to drink of this water of perfect contemplation whenever we like: the choice is not ours. This divine union is something quite supernatural, given that it may cleanse the soul and leave it pure and free from the mud and misery in which it has been plunged because of its sins. . . . In contemplation the Lord calls souls to his side at once, and in a single moment reveals more truths to them and gives them a clearer insight into the nature of everything than they could otherwise gain in many years. . . . Remember, the Lord invites us all" (*Way of Perfection* XIX).

It is as if the waters have bathed our eyes to remove the film of false vision, and now we see as God sees—vast perspectives somehow encapsulated in one flash of pure insight. Yet it is hard, or even impossible, to express such intuitive "visions" in words. They are too comprehensive, and the wisdom they reveal in an instant of illumination is beyond the ponderous searchings and recapitulations of the human intellect. Only the mystics, by the use of figurative language, manage to convey some of what the Spirit has shown them.

Near the end of her life Teresa wrote (*Interior Castle,* VII, iii), "For from those divine breasts, where it seems that God is ever sustaining the soul, flow streams of milk, which solace all who dwell in the Castle." The contemplative receives the "streams of milk" directly from the Spirit, who causes them to flow out in "a stream of this [living] water, to sustain those who in bodily matters have to serve the Bridegroom and the bride."

The Bridegroom is Christ, the bride his church, and Teresa is telling us how the soul bathed in the living waters prayer is used by Jesus to channel his blessings to others so that we are all united together in him in mutual, caring help and love.

"There is a river whose streams refresh the city of God, and it sanctifies the dwelling of the Most High. God is inside the city—she can never fall" (Ps 46).

In a sense, the waters are tidal, for they ebb and flow in us, as does our level of awareness of their presence and action. Yet, even in periods of apparent blankness, we never reach that stage of gasping aridity that afflicted us in the deep purgations. Always there remains an indefinable certainty that the river is there, that it flows, that we drink of it, that it will now never dry up within us. At such times it is as if we were resting in a spartan bed during a moonless night, yet we can still see the multitude of stars outside our window and hear the gentle swishing and gurgling sounds of a river flowing purposefully along only a few yards away at the bottom of our garden.

We are sure the Beloved will again summon us there for us to drink and bathe, but this is for him to decide. We are content to rest in peace, waiting, for the hour of his choice.

John of the Cross writes, "And thus this spirit of God, while hidden in the veins of the soul, is like sweet and delectable water quenching the thirst of the spirit; and when the soul offers the sacrifice of love to God, it becomes living flames of fire, which are the lamps of the act of love" (*Living Flame* III, 8). John deliciously mixes his metaphors, but the total effect is one of liquid glory and transfiguration in the risen Lord.

The experiential inundations of the living waters are not necessary either for sanctity or for an effective apostolate. They are extras that have dynamic consequences in our lives, and, by extension, in those of others, just by being there in the purity bestowed by the Spirit's permeation.

The divine life of the Trinity is one of circumincession—a constant interflow of ineffable love and communion among the Three-in-one. This cyclic flow was extended to us when Mary said yes to the angel and the Son became also her Son, and our Lord, choosing to be one with us in all things except sin.

The trillions upon trillions of human beings who have existed on this earth from the beginning till now, and the others who will follow till the end time, have each a definite, in-built, personal capacity for receiving the living waters. Fulfillment for one would be painful inadequacy for another; the huge abundance that one can contain would annihilate someone else. Individual fulfillment in the third syndrome comes when our capacity is exactly matched with the measure of living waters, or divine life, that the Creator made us capable of receiving and containing.

If we consider all the ways in which water is present to us, we can find analogies for the living waters prayer.

Think of Niagara or Victoria Falls, the great thundering might of them, and see them as a symbol of the force of God's love cascading upon humanity and bearing all before it. The heart responds with awe and gratitude at this exuberance of giving. It praises and worships him before such compelling evidence of his beauty, and so the heart enters the living waters prayer.

Think of a fountain ceaselessly playing, but cascading upward instead of down as in Niagara. See how it leaps toward light and sky, how its waters glitter in rainbow patterns as the sun catches the myriad drops. See the graceful curves as they turn at their highest point to stream down again, keeping the pool at the fountain's base full.

The fountain is a figure for our prayer of love and delight spontaneously leaping up to the Trinity. And yet that Trinity is itself the source of the prayer, as the pool is the source of the fountain waters. The cyclic nature of the prayer of living waters is symbolized by their continuously rising and falling circuit. The rainbow mosaics of light and color that they make are like the arrow prayers of joy and thanksgiving at God's very existence that the Spirit arouses in the transformed heart. The fountain plays on and on, even while we are asleep, or preoccupied with work, or interacting with other people, or enjoying some leisure pursuit. Its waters circulate through all these activities, though we are not consciously aware of this. Once our will is to live for God and to be a conduit for his love, he draws up this fountain within us, and himself controls its playing.

We could think also of lakes—the remote ones of the wilderness areas, bushed to their shores, mirroring skies, moonlight, sunshine, a flight of birds, a trout leaping, a skimming kingfisher.

We are awed by their great depths, many of them filling ancient glacier and river valleys between mountains. We contemplate the silence, darkness, stillness of those depths, their secrets and their chill.

They symbolize our own inner depths, those hidden, unplumbed canyons where God lives in us. The lake's surface is our upper consciousness where his glories are mirrored in our life, his living water sustaining the myriad forms of the expression of our mutual love.

The mystery of these enormous pools of inner blessedness entrances us. We wonder at God's inscrutability and lower ourselves in trust and peace into the numinous to float there, the living waters effortlessly supporting us.

The imagery and analogies for the living waters are inexhaustible, as are the ways in which it expresses itself through our lives, actions and prayer. God invites us to come, drink, immerse ourselves, and then let him draw us down, down into those inexhaustible, mysterious depths. Do we draw back in fear of the consequences? Or do we give ourselves to those waters and let them do what they will with us?

At conception God planted in us a certain capacity for receiving and transmitting the living waters. If we never fulfill this potential we enter eternity unable to live the fullness of glory and union intended for us. Our purgatory will be to see what we have missed, and then have no option but to accept the second, or hundredth best, that is all we agreed to receive in this life, and is now our portion forever.

A PLACE TO PUT THINGS

It is like a mine shaft
plunging to untold depths.
You can let things drop into it
and know you will never see them again.
I don't mean rubbish
or weapons of war like guns and bombs—
I mean things far too precious
to be left lying about up above
where they might get trampled on
stolen, desecrated, lost, defaced—
    a love too holy to be fulfilled,
    the memory of a moment outside time,
    a longing that makes nonsense of your daily life,
    a blessing that never reached its destination,
    words unspoken,
    enrichment denied—
            or else their opposites.

You crane over that passage into darkness,
you let fall your precious treasures
one by one or in a glittering heap.
They tumble out of sight.
You hear no sound of landfall.
    The shaft is bottomless
    a plunging wound once made in time
    now centered in eternity.
            Your offerings are safe forever.

COME IN

Heaven is within, he said.

Then let us go inside
and seek this emptiness
that is the fullness
of all being,
this no-thing
in which is total plenitude.

The way in is like a gash
cut in a rock face.
You have to let the knife slash
to open up this place
before you can go in.

Then comes the arduous journey
explorers know about—
the unexpected caverns of delight,
the narrow tunnels
(constricting birth canals),
the lack of light,
the water flowing, dripping, gurgling,
in negating dark—
living waters everywhere in runnels
and the starkness
of unyielding rock, and pain
of body and its bones
crushed between huge stones.

But if we go together
we are not alone.
A helpmate on this journey
shortens all its span, speeds up
its arduous initiation process,
telescopes time and space
so that in one swift leap

we both arrive together
at that longed-for place
that is no-place
but total being,
instant seeing,
dissolving in embrace,
knowing face to face.

The Prayer
of Heightened
Awareness
—A Personal Witness

In this prayer certain truths that we believe and hold to in faith become, through a special grace, a lived actuality for us. We are made acutely, consciously aware that what we believe *is so*.

The *pleroma,* fullness of presence, is one of the risen Lord's attributes, expressed through his Spirit. It is "the fullness of him who fills the universe in all its parts" (Eph 1:23), and who passes on this fullness to "all of us" through his grace (Jn 1:16). Or, as the Good News Bible has it, "Out of the fullness of his grace he has blessed us all, giving us one blessing after another." Another way of expressing it is to affirm that "All things have been subjected to the Son so that God may be All in all" (1 Cor 15:28), sharing his munificence with us in various ways in the third syndrome and through the Son's resurrection love-life.

As Paul boldly puts it, "There is only Christ. He is everything and he is in everything" (Col 3:11).

The prayer of heightened awareness is given us through our response to certain aspects of the pleroma to convince us of the above truths. Pan-en-theism (which is distinct from pantheism) recognizes the immanence of God in nature, and is aware of his presence in, and his holding in being of, the beauties and wonders of nature. When this awareness is intensified by a special grace given briefly, it is as if we saw these for the first time, as on Eden morning before corruption had dulled our awareness of the flawless glory of creation.

Sometimes, especially in the resurrection love-life state, we perceive one particular divine Person, or the whole Trinity, in this way. The experience of the indwelling within our own soul has then expanded to focus vividly upon its reality in some other aspect of creation. Such awarenesses cannot be self-induced, and parodies of them that occur in conjunction with the taking of certain drugs are not Spirit-filled, or forms of, graced prayer.

In the genuine heightened awareness it is as if the risen, glorified Lord and his dancing Spirit are plainly glimpsed (though not with physical eyes in a "vision") and experienced directly and unexpectedly in places or people. The result is spontaneous awe, praise and adoration like Jacob's after his dream at Bethel.

Our hearts cry out in reverence and exaltation, "Truly, God is in this place and I never knew it! How awe-inspiring this place is! This is nothing less than a house of God. This is the gate of heaven" (Gen 28:16–17).

We are aware that here in this particular place or person is "God's house," and it is therefore holy and to be reverenced. We have been graced to enter briefly into that heavenly state where God is experienced as being "All in all," which is to be our final destiny after death.

It is as if an immense spiritual horizon has opened up and in the eternal light radiating from it we "see" the whole of creation, or specific aspects of it, as completely penetrated by Trinitarian glory and holiness. We could not bear such intensity of vision for long, and so the Spirit partially veils our sight again, and yet through that veil the glory glimmers like the aurora borealis in the night sky or the afterglow from the sunset. The fluctuations in intensity are inevitable, given the nature of the receiving apparatus.

Precisely because we are human and necessarily involved in the practicalities of the world we live in, our awareness of the indwelling in all its forms is usually muted or even unconscious, welling up to possess us consciously only at Spirit-chosen times of special blessing and grace.

A personal account follows of such a grace of heightened awareness given me some twenty years ago, but still vivid in my mind as uniquely holy and compelling.

It was winter—if benign Auckland can ever be said to have a winter. It was early afternoon, a day of clear sunlight, cold wind and glittering air. I had gone to Cornwall Park, that reserve of hundreds of acres given to the city by one of its early pioneers. Here, surrounding the high volcanic hill in its center, are clumps and avenues of a variety of trees, native and exotic. Here are walking tracks and rolling paddocks where sheep graze. Here it is possible to be alone with God in the middle of the city, and here I was used to coming when the longing was upon me.

This sunny winter's afternoon I went to a favorite place—a knoll in a large green paddock. From where I stood the land sloped away in gentle undulations to the distant tree-lined drive and the busy streets. The sun was inclining toward the northwest so that it shone directly upon the long, informal grove of gnarled olive trees that meandered for a kilometer to the flat place well below. Their silvery, graceful movements in the wind were always a special delight to me, so this day I stood on the knoll at the head of the slope and gazed across at them with acute pleasure. There was no other human being in sight.

As I contemplated their festive dance, my delight became imbued with a different quality of response. God gave me a direct awareness of the truth about the olive trees—the truth that Father, Son and Spirit are present in all creation, holding it in being, endowing it with life, energy, beauty, wonder and fathomless spirituality, the origin and crown of which we shall know in heaven when we see God face to face.

It was as if the risen Christ himself was dancing exultantly and the trees in the wind had become his vehicle of expression. He was "playing" them as a musician plays his chosen instrument. They

had become olive trees of heaven—eternal trees whose glory would
never fade. Through them Jesus was performing a bridegroom's
nuptial dance for me, his bride.

As the boughs and leaves glanced and gleamed and tossed in
the silvery sunshine, I knew him present in them telling me, "You
are my chosen beloved, and all this beauty is my gift for you. I lift
you up into my dance of consummated bliss. My radiance is yours.
My glory flows out into you, and so you shine for me."

His lissome grace was permeating his creation, concentrated
for me in this moment before the grove of olive trees. His healing
hands had touched my eyes so that, in a spiritual sense, they were
opened and I "saw" the reality of creation.

> In the beginning was the Word;
> the Word was with God
> and the Word was God.
> He was with God in the beginning.
> *Through him all things came to be,*
> *not one thing had its being but through him.*
> *All that came to be had life in him*
> and that life was the light of men,
> a light that shines in the dark,
> a light that darkness could not overpower (Jn 1:1–5).

There had never been any darkness in the olive trees and never
would be on that transcendent plane on which I had been shown
them. And I too, in my inner, graced self, was lifted up in exaltation
where the risen Lord was directly experienced as All in all.

As I stood there, entranced, tears of bliss sliding down my face,
I danced in spirit with the olive trees, the beloved partner of the
Lord in whose being they had originated, and whose beauty they
were manifesting. I "saw" my own inner essence as part of what the
Lord had made and kept in being. I was one with him, and with all
his creation, and he and it were one with me. His Spirit permeated
and hallowed all that had been made through him. I understood
how Moses had felt before the burning bush of glory that flamed
and yet was not consumed, and what made Peter, James and John,
when they saw Jesus transfigured on Hermon, fall on their faces in

dread, wonder and worship. What was eternal could never cease to be. It was the Reality behind all the partial, distorted realities that make up the major part of our lives.

I knew why God had told Moses to take off his shoes, for he stood on a holy place.

I myself was standing on sheep-cropped grasses and gazing at olive trees that were holy emanations of the Divine Lover rejoicing and dancing in his creation.

After what was probably only a few minutes, yet seemed time-less, the heightened awareness faded, and the olive trees were once more only olive trees, and yet I knew they were holy. An extra dimension of knowledge and love had been infused into me and its fruits have been permanent.

Soon afterward, I wrote this poem:

> Green, cropped grass
> busy, grazing sheep
> undulating field
> like gentle spillway from a rustic dam.
>
> Here I
> arrested by your call
> here fronting the olive trees
> stood and gazed.
>
> The grove descended with the field.
> I saw tossed wave on tossing wave
> of softly silvered leaves
> stirring and rocking
> seething with the wind
> trunks like knotted ropes
> tarred, tortured, twisted into wicks. . . .
>
> The trees are dancing
> for a wedding day.
> They celebrate with ballerina grace
> your presence in their boughs.

No burning brand this light
that ripples silver as they ebb and flow
that shimmers softly as they pulse and whirl
that swirls in billows as they swing and surge.

"Stand here," you tell me,
"while I teach you
the olive trees of heaven manifesting joy."

You catch me up and rock me with the trees
you hide me in their silver-green recesses
you pour this soft light in a cascade on my brow
you twine its tresses all about my face.
You kiss me in the stir of flurrying leaves
you touch me with the wand of your delight
you bend and catch me up into your bliss.

I stand here
still
while tears slide on my cheeks.

I gaze upon the vision, con the code,
rapt as you show me who you are
and why you made these trees
and what it is they glance and gleam about.

Our wedding guests
are dancing for the feast.
Soft swathes of halo gossamer
reflect the radiance that is your face.
I look upon the trees
and see your face.

You crown me where I wait
here in the green field, alert
and listening as you speak.
This celebration

of the frosted olive trees
with light and wind
hosannahs you.

I see you lissome.

Grave beatitude
exalts my fragile clay. You lave me
in its rapture as you pass.

And then you go.

Time and again I have been given a heightened awareness of
the indwelling in Christed people I have been close to in spiritual
love. This is a sublime, exquisite experience, especially when it
is mutual. I have also "seen" Jesus crucified in some people—
especially in one unbelieving person who most bitterly maligned
the Catholic Church and cruelly persecuted a close member of his
family who was converted to its doctrines.

I have also been given awareness of Christ suffering in many
afflicted people (including myself). He has called out to me piteous-
ly from within them and I have been torn with compassion. Where
it was possible, I succored the suffering Lord there where he was,
but often the circumstances make this impossible. Then all I can do
is pray and empathize.

For example, recently I was walking in the main street of our
little country town and saw coming toward me a woman pushing
a kind of wheelchair-cum-pram. In this vehicle was crunched up a
travesty of a man—hunchbacked, the size of a ten year old boy, but
with the face of an adult, his feet and legs doubled up, his hands and
arms distorted, his head enlarged.

And yet he was no idiot. There was intelligence and awareness
of his plight in his face. He knew what he was—one of nature's cruel
mistakes, a freak, one doomed to be dependent on others till he
died, the normal satisfactions and activities of normal life denied
him.

I wanted to put my arms around him and say, "I love you," for

I knew Jesus was imprisoned with him in that black joke of a body—but we passed, going opposite directions, as so often happens in life.

I am certain that many, whose vocation it is to succor the afflicted, often also in their compassionate, caring love are given the grace of heightened awareness of Jesus suffering in their charges, though maybe they never realize the grace for what it is. All they know is that they love these suffering ones almost unbearably, and are compelled to cherish them in a practical way.

Heightened awareness may also be given through perhaps dramatic endorsement of some truth of the faith. Here is another personal example.

At a time preceding by some years that of the olive trees, I was given what was a heightened awareness of sin, and its effects both on Jesus and on humanity. I have been deeply influenced by what I "saw" then, and it did much to shape my spirituality by drawing me compulsively to choose to participate in the Savior's redemptive work. This was in a specific way about which the Spirit continued to enlighten me more and more deeply right up to the present time, over thirty years later.

At this period in my life, not long after my conversion and reception into the church, I had been and still was reading deeply in doctrine. What I read about the origins and nature of sin had given me many insights into matters, personal and universal, that had puzzled and troubled me for years. (Later, these "showings" crystallized into the concept of what I called the first syndrome: Sin/Suffering/Evil.)

One dank, cold winter's morning I emerged by the church's side door from an early morning Sunday mass to see before me the familiar vista of the Catholic boys' schoolyard and muddy playing fields with a stand of tall, dark trees beyond, and, past that, suburbia.

The air was full of the dampness of unshed rain, everything was sodden and dripping from overnight downpours, and the sky was threateningly gray and overcast. The only relief to all this drabness was straight before me, beyond the playing fields, where a low winter's sun was striving to show itself through a few slits in the clouds. The creamy light was the sole cheerful sign in the whole vista.

Then, all in an instant, as I paused there on the step, I "saw" the whole world steeped in sin, the glory of God's creation, both of nature and humankind, infiltrated and soiled by an evil, hostile force that was chillingly malicious and real. I "saw" the Satanic element oozing out from its dark, mysterious source, like gray rain from sullen skies, to thwart God's salvific intention. The awfulness of the threat to humanity, of the presence of evil in the form of the collective blight of "original sin" rooted deep down in each of us, as well as the personal sin of us all throughout the ages, horrified me. The awareness of it as one threatening whole was intense.

Here was a diabolic invitation to despair, and the dread it aroused in me was overpowering.

Mercifully, after two or three minutes the heightened awareness vanished, and there before me was only a soggy, New Zealand winter's morning making me want to get home quickly out of the cold and the rain, and light the fire.

However, the experience left me with an indelible conviction that sin was a reality, that because of it we had to have a Savior, and that in his passion he had consented to have the whole filthy pile of it heaped upon himself so that he "became sin" for us. It also convinced me that he was calling me to be a "sin-taker" with him and share that vile load for love of him and my neighbor in whatever way he chose for me.

Throughout this book I have laid stress on the spiritual actuality of the divine indwelling. We believe in it in faith, but at times God blesses us with a grace of heightened awareness of its presence. This may be given in relation to one or all three of the divine Persons. Most often it is in the form of a call to and awareness of vivid union with Jesus in one or other of his mysteries. In the state of resurrection love-life this awareness is mostly centered on his resurrected and ascended state.

To me, during my early years in the church, it came countless times in relation to the sufferings of his passion—as one watching and praying in agony with him in Gethsemane; as a cross-bearer, another Simon of Cyrene, toiling up Calvary and keeping him company as I shared with him the pain, shame, humiliation, and superhuman physical effort of that journey; as a participant in his utter poverty as he was stripped and hoisted up naked before the jeering crowd; as a co-worker in the final redemptive task of abandonment and dereliction on the cross; and after all this, an entering into the death-state with him and a lying spiritually inert and frozen for years, sharing his entombment.

Later came the heightened awareness of rising with him and the exultant, joyous love-union of the resurrection love-life sharing.

Such interpenetrations on the spiritual level make the truths of the faith indelible, and the reality of Jesus in both his humanity and his divinity absolutely convincing.

Graces of heightened awareness can also occur in a way that finally convinces us of the reality of the indwelling in others, and that it truly does weld us all into one body, the mystical body of Christ, united in his Spirit of love. We may directly experience the presence of the Lord in any of these: an intimate, most beloved friend-in-Christ; a family member; a neighbor we are barely acquainted with; someone we have known for years (and yet never really "known") and now suddenly "see" for the first time; the lonely, the afflicted, the physically ill; the mentally and emotionally tortured; the unwanted and despised . . .

There is no human being, through all the spectrum from hardened sinner to great saint, in whom we cannot "see" Christ as he lives out his mysteries through them, but it remains a special grace that must be "given." To illustrate this, I will cite one brief, simple, yet compelling incident that has remained vividly in my mind, as all experiences of heightened awareness do.

Years ago, during one of my stays in the hospital, I wandered into another ward once I was well enough to get out of bed and walk around. In the first bed I came to there was an elderly, very frail woman lying on her back, wide awake, but obviously ill and suffering. Spontaneously drawn to her, I went and stood by the bed, lifted into mine the veined old hand lying on the coverlet, and smiled into her eyes. She smiled back into mine as if in recognition, though we had never seen each other before. Then she said in her tired, faint voice, "We'll meet again, dear."

We smiled lovingly, pressed hands, and I went away.

That was all that happened, yet in that few minutes of mostly silent interchange, each of us was given a grace of heightened awareness of Christ's presence in the other. This mutual recognition, wordless and instantaneous, was delicately and most beautifully spiritual. We both silently acknowledged that we would indeed "meet again"—in heaven, where we would see face-to-face the beloved Lord who momentarily revealed to us how we were united in him in the here and now.

Here was another profound affirmation of a basic truth of the Christian faith, shared at a deeply spiritual level, and providing mutual reassurance, hope and courage to go on enduring.

Through such prayers of heightened awareness God bestows on us special graces of intuitive—not intellectual—knowledge and discernment. Later they can be interpreted and explicated by the intellect, but at the time we simply "know" beyond any words and concepts the mind can devise. The unfathomable message is directly infused, in all its mystery, into the depths of the soul. From there it will from time to time surge up to illuminate thought and gently direct action. Usually it goes on bearing such fruits of conscious, shaping insight for years.

This kind of prayer is a logical development from our baptismal incorporation into the whole Christ. God gives us faith—which John of the Cross tells us is "thick darkness to the understanding" and Paul says is "the evidence of things not seen"—and this enables us to apprehend obscurely and believe tenaciously mysteries incomprehensible to the ungraced intellect.

Through such faith we affirm what is there even though we do not experience it in any direct, definable manner. As faith deepens through trials and purifications we become more often aware of God's hidden presence within us (and others) and rely upon it more and more. In transforming union, the shadowy awareness is constant and permanent. We live with and in the arms of a Presence. We have only to turn from the outside in to rest in its secret actuality. This affirmation in blind faith is the ordinary state of Christian union with the Trinity.

However, when he chooses, and to whom he chooses, and with no reference to human assessments of worthiness or unworthiness, God grants times of heightened awareness through which new dimensions of conscious experience and intuitive knowledge and affirmation are added to the obscure faith. Though we can predispose ourselves to receive this prayer, we cannot make it for ourselves. It is a grace, and the disposal of it remains with God alone, though our own proven openness to receive divine action, no matter in what form it chooses to express itself or whether the results are painful or pleasant to us personally, facilitates matters.

In other words, the more habitually and deeply we are abandoned and receptive, the simpler it is for God to infuse such special graces into us—but he still chooses whom he wills.

Creation is everywhere. God is everywhere and in everyone. He made all things through Christ. His Spirit holds them all in being and directs the course of events and our own growth in holiness. It is our own level of awareness that is inadequate, and must be so at least to some degree, unless God himself chooses to raise it, for we are merely human, and of the earth earthy. Only grace can lift us above that level, and it is God who controls grace, not we.

THE WAY IN

A window to look out of
is enough. Even a single
blade of grass, if only
one knew the way in
to its private mystery.

Or these two birds that dart
in mating frenzy overhead.
Or one straight frond
flicked upward at its tip
in urgency of that young pine's
spring growth and aspiration.

Or one look from your blue
and honest eyes that
meeting mine
do not waver, but remain
locked in steadfast
and unblinking pledge.

Any one of these could be
the Way, the Truth, the Life.

The Abba Prayer

"Abba" is the Jewish equivalent of our English "daddy"—an intimate, loving, trusting way of addressing a father you are so certain loves you dearly that you never have cause to question that love. To call God "daddy" may seem to some irreverent and distastefully familiar, yet it is the term Jesus himself used for his Father, and he did so both in everyday life and in the extremity of his Gethsemane trial of trust. As children of God, we ourselves surely find the term exactly appropriate as our abba-prayer reply to his loving reassurances. There are few more touching metaphors for this than what Jesus said in Matthew 10:29–31: "Can you not buy two sparrows for a penny? And yet not one falls to the ground without your Father knowing. Why, every hair on your head has been counted. So there is no need to be afraid; you are worth more than hundreds of sparrows."

The fatherhood of God is a familiar scriptural theme, explicit in many psalms, in the gospels and in Paul's letters. Perhaps Jesus summed it up most powerfully yet simply and movingly, in the parable of the prodigal son, whose father actually ran to meet and embrace him "while yet he was a long way off" and before he had even had a chance to say he was sorry.

Like any caring father who yearns over a delinquent child, our Abba never ceases to long for our homecoming. He is prepared to do anything at all to bring it about, even to accepting imprisonment in a human body and confinement in our limited time and space, even to enduring intolerable suffering and a monstrously unjust, excruciating death for our sakes. In human, colloquial terms, we would have to say that our Abba is "crazy about" us, his children.

Whatever we do, however we flout him, he will welcome us back with outstretched arms the moment he sees we have ceased rushing away from him, made an about turn, and begun our journey back home.

All lovers of God who have given him their whole allegiance and trust practice the abba prayer in one way or another. Its presence is signified by childlike trust, a high degree of abandonment, an experiential knowledge of divine cherishing and tenderness, and an endless gratitude for the Father's loving care that is so evident in one's life—even under the disguise of various forms of suffering and apparent defeat. The conviction of God's absolute goodness, power and love is an indelible part of the abba prayer. The certainty that he knows what he is about, no matter what the circumstances through which he presents his will, comes spontaneously, and a peaceful act of abandonment occurs with it.

When Jesus used the abba prayer he revealed a personal relationship that both reflected the very best of human father-son mutual love, and the awareness that the nurturing capacities of his own heavenly Father infinitely surpassed those of any earthly parent. He also made plain in his teachings that, as he and his Father are "in" one another and so indissolubly united, and as we, his disciples, have been made one with him by our loving obedience to his will, we also share in his abba union with his Father. "You will understand that I am in my Father and you in me and I in you" (Jn 14:20).

The Abba's love channels itself through the Son to reach us, and so reveals its qualities in a human way. Jesus longed to gather the wayward people of Jerusalem into his care just as a hen gathered her chicks under her wings—only they refused him. Those who have watched a hen doing this, with gentle, reassuring, inviting clucks, and seen the tiny, fluffy chicks disappear into the downy soft haven she provides, will know what an endearingly homely analogy Jesus used. It has all kinds of undertones of tenderness and maternal succoring. Since Jesus is comparing himself to the hen, he is indicating that he—and by extension, the Father—possesses precisely these maternal, nurturing qualities and longs to express them toward us. Leading on from this, the love-starved, inner child in us would be soothed and healed by calling God "mommy" as well as "daddy." If we are humble and little enough, we shall be able to do this.

The abba prayer is always uttered by one who has experienced in his or her relationship with God such surpassing tenderness. "A weaned child on its mother's breast, even so is my soul" (Ps 130:2). And, "It was you who created my being, knit me together in my mother's womb" (Ps 138:13). Even as we floated in amniotic fluid, helpless and dependent upon our mother for everything, our Abba's love cradled us and knew and formed our precious individuality. Each of us was his chosen, unique new life whose destiny he had in his care before ever we were born—indeed, before "ever we came to be." Whatever adverse effects there were of heredity and environment, he had already taken into consideration and made his plans about, asking only that we love and trust him enough to let him steer us safely home to him through them all.

Scripture repeatedly reveals the abba relationship to us. Paul tells us: "Everyone moved by the Spirit is a son [or daughter] of God. The spirit you received is not the spirit of slaves bringing fear into your lives again—it is the spirit of sons [and daughters], and it makes us cry out, 'Abba, Father!' The Spirit himself and our spirit bear united witness that we are children of God. And if we are children, we are heirs as well: heirs of God and coheirs with Christ, sharing his sufferings so as to share his glory" (Rom 8:14–17).

Here the Trinity affirm the abba relationship and make plain some of the characteristics of the prayer flowing from it. The Spirit initiates it, infusing knowledge of what it entails. There is no fear in it, in the sense of a slave's fear of a cruel, punitive master. We are not God's slaves (except in the sense that we willingly turn our whole selves and lives over to him to use as he wills). We are legitimately born into his family. We have the rights and privileges of beloved daughters and sons who know they belong where they are. This certainty does not make them arrogant and conceited but docile and grateful, just as Jesus was. Both he and we are heirs to all of God's endless riches of grace and strength and power, but we must face the fact that being a coheir with Christ means being one with the *whole* Christ, not just those aspects for which we feel a warmly sentimental attraction. Being an intimate, truly belonging member of the family means sharing both the glory and the suffering of the Son.

The abba prayer is one of God the Father's gifts to us, and our exemplar is Jesus in all his mysteries—the extended incarnation, the continuous passion, the resurrection love-life and the triumph of the ascension. He lives in us, and so all these are ours as well as his.

But we also share in the humble, hidden aspects—the helpless dependence of his infancy and early childhood, his being cherished and protected by Joseph, and, through Joseph by his heavenly Abba, the unfolding in a concealed way of his destiny through his adolescence and early manhood in the uneventful life of Nazareth— daily work and sharing of a simple, homely, human existence with his human parents. Through his mother Mary, he entered deeply into the motherliness of his Abba and absorbed them into his own nature to share them with us. He knew from personal experience what human mothering meant in all its beauty as it issued from the only perfect mother humanity has known. It enriched his abba prayer with countless mysteries of intuitive wisdom and under-standing and wordless ways of conveying the depths of tender, caring love and empathy.

If we think of Jesus incarnate as a baby in a human mother, and so often embraced and comforted by that mother and his foster father, we see how real the abba prayer must have been to him. He was indeed a tiny baby, a toddler, a four year old, a young boy adventuring, getting hurt, playing vigorous games with other boys, feeling lonely and bemused about his future at times—and always when he turned to his parents they were there to cherish and com-fort. He learned what his divine Abba's love and nurturing were like through their human cherishing. To think of him in those early years with his head held against her breast by his mother, or being lifted up in Joseph's strong, protective arms and held tight, gives us the perfect concrete image of the abba prayer, and of what later, in his teachings and actions, he sought to convey to us about trust in and abandonment to God's will expressed through the moment-by-moment action of divine providence.

God the Father loved his Son through the human parents he had provided for him. Jesus advanced in grace and wisdom as he grew to maturity, patterning himself on Mary and Joseph, while he responded in loving gratitude to their nurturing. None of us is provided with a sinless mother, and with a father holy enough to be entrusted with looking after her and her divine Son. Our parents are like us—flawed in their innermost selves by the tendency to pull away from God, to flout his will, and to fall far short of perfect love for him or for any human being, including ourselves.

And yet we do find a way through their loving care of us into the experience of the abba prayer. Alternatively and sadly, many of those who are unloved, unwanted and abused as children find it impossible even to believe in God, let alone in a heavenly Father who is all love and compassion. And yet it can and does happen that such disastrous early lives have the opposite effect of driving their victims into an abba relationship with God the Father, or sometimes with a human substitute the quality of whose love leads them to their Abba, just because of their agonizing lack of it at the human level.

In the abba relationship with God, of which the abba prayer is an essential part, we are helped if we can take our own inner child, whether wounded or sound, in our own arms and offer it to God as Joseph and Mary offered Jesus in the temple in the presence of Simeon. It is sometimes easier to do this than to offer our specifically adult self. This is so because a child's instinctive need in trouble and when threatened is to run to the refuge of its father's or mother's arms. As adults we have "passed that stage" we feel, and so do not as humbly and readily run to God, certain of safety and protection.

We can learn a lot from St. Thérèse of Lisieux. The Holy Spirit gave her insight on how to spiritualize her inward child, and she had the courage and strength of character to capitalize on the weaknesses of her child. Our inner child may well take us by the hand and teach us too, if only we let her.

One of the plainest examples of Thérèse's deliberately childlike trust put into action occurred when she was appointed novice mistress when barely twenty herself.

In her manuscript dedicated to Mother Marie de Gonzague, she writes: "I was to work in the hallowed ground of souls. I saw at once that this was beyond my powers, so I went to God in the spirit of a child that throws itself into its father's arms, and nestles its head against his shoulder. 'Lord,' I said, 'I'm such a poor thing—I haven't got it in me to give these children of yours their food. If you want each of them to get what she needs, you'll have to put it here, in my hand. I'm not going to leave your arms, I'm not going to turn my head and look at them; I'll simply pass on what you give me to each soul that comes to me for its food" (*Autobiography of a Saint,* p. 283).

Such an advanced degree of trust and evidence of infused wisdom are sure signs of the state of transforming union. In Thérèse resurrection love-life was so fully developed, even though she was so young, that she was able to get right out of God's way, placing her inward child in his arms to receive his messages for her, and then she carried them out in the spirit of that child. She put no barrier of self-will in her Abba's path. Though most children have plenty of self-will, she went to her Abba to "nestle her head against his shoulder" and rest there in unconcerned submission. Her child self then unquestioningly transmitted what his will required of the adult Thérèse who was waiting to carry it out and promptly did so.

Human beings can have few more satisfying and pacifying experiences of being loved and protected than that found when, as children, they "nestled" in a parent's arms—relaxed, safe, enfolded, cherished. In such a situation spiritually experienced with our heavenly Father, our Abba, how can we help but respond with trust and willingness to obey, no matter what?

This abba prayer of the inner child who is conscious of God's protection is obviously closely allied to the prayers of embrace and resting in God examined earlier in this book.

There is in most of us, sometimes buried deep, sometimes near the surface and fully operative, a child. If it is a happy child, fulfilled as it should be by loving and being loved, exploring the world confidently, playing, snuggling into its parents' arms sure that it is cherished and valued, then it remains a positive force in our adult lives. It keeps us young in heart, with the ability to enjoy all kinds of play, using the word in its widest and constructive sense. It gives us a permanently trusting, affirmative attitude to life and people. It does not inhibit our growth toward emotional maturity, but fosters it through its capacity for spontaneous enjoyment, childlike wonder at creation, openness to experience, and lack of free-floating anxiety.

By contrast, if our child is miserable and has a fretful sense of being unloved, unwanted, unappreciated, unaffirmed and unsafe, then we have trouble on our hands, and so do other people. Such an inward child influencing a chronologically mature person is evidenced by various forms of emotional immaturity in that adult's attitudes and behavior, especially in personal relationships. Invariably the source of this arrested emotional development will be found in inadequate nurturing of one or several kinds in the early years, and the basic symptom from which most of the other problems derive is a pervasive sense of insecurity. And feeling insecure arises from an inability to trust, and vice versa.

This psychological problem of compulsive mistrust can be remedied finally and fully only in the development of a high level of trust in God—that is, if we are considering the problem from the spiritual as well as the emotional angle. However many human relationships we may have in which mutual trust is a factor, it can never be perfect trust, for all humans are imperfect. This includes even canonized saints. St. Philip Neri's prayer sums it up: "My God, beware of Philip, else he will betray thee."

This bleak awareness of the basic untrustworthiness of all human beings, including ourselves, is necessary for the development of perfect trust in God, for it impels us toward dependence on his love and grace because we make such a mess of things when we try "to go it alone." Our Abba's love, in contrast to human love, is flawless, and forever.

In a way, those afflicted with emotional insecurity are at an advantage spiritually once they recognize and understand their state and then turn to God as Abba in their inadequacy and possible desperation. If, through the abba prayer, they expose their deep-seated heart-wound to God's love, healing and sanctification of a crippling psychological condition is initiated. "My grace is sufficient for you. My strength is made perfect in your weakness" (2 Cor 19:9). Our Abba's healing is his "free gift to us in the Beloved" (Eph 1:6), our part being to yearn for and open ourselves to receive that gift through the practice of the abba prayer.

Jesus was not speaking lightly or sentimentally when he warned "solemnly" that "unless you change and become like little children you will never enter the kingdom of heaven" (Mt 18:3). Those are strong words. Such "little ones" have, as their hallmark, "faith in" Jesus, and we are never to despise any of them or harm them. Those who do, he warns, are in for dire consequences. Obviously Jesus cannot be referring only to children under five. He must be indicating the simplicity of the trusting love that children at this stage and age give their parents, and how necessary it is for us adults to have the same attitude to him and to his and our Abba.

Later he reiterates that the kingdom of heaven belongs to such "little children" and they are not to be stopped from approaching him (Mt 19:14). We "stop" ourselves and others from coming to Jesus in childlike trust and simplicity when we mock them for their unworldliness and naiveté, try to make them see a number of points of view instead of their chosen one of "God alone," and confuse them with "ifs", "buts", "shoulds" and "should nots" when all they want to do is simply love unquestioningly.

We harm their trust when we infer that God is like a stern, much-preoccupied father, absorbed in important business deals, who must not be interrupted by our asking him to attend to our trivial affairs. We do even worse harm when we let the Devil of Negativity infer that our Abba is punitive and cruel, vigilantly on the alert for us to make one wrong move so that he can pounce, punish us with rejection in his rage ("God won't love you if you do that! He'll send you to hell"), and destroy our trust by harping on our wickedness and vileness.

Here again Thérèse can help us with our abba prayer. She herself had certainly suffered emotional traumas in her early life. These left her with a wounded, love-needy inward child. Through the Holy Spirit's enlightenments she learned how to spiritualize her emotional problems by offering her child self unreservedly to God. In this she was certainly helped by the fact that, irrespective of traumas, she had had a deeply loving, trustful relationship with her human father. This obviously provided a basis for her later heroically positive attitude to her heavenly Father.

Seeing herself so weak and imperfect, she did not waste time beating her breast and dramatizing the situation. Instead she found her remedy in scripture.

In her manuscript dedicated to Mother Marie de Gonzague she wrote: "Obviously there's nothing great to be made of me, so it must be possible for me to aspire to sanctity in spite of my insignificance. I've got to take myself just as I am, with all my imperfections; but somehow I shall have to find out a little way, all of my own, which will be a direct short-cut to heaven. After all (I said to myself) we live in an age of inventions. Nowadays, people don't even bother to climb the stairs—rich people, anyhow; they find a lift more convenient. Can't I find a lift which will take me up to Jesus, since I'm not big enough to climb the steep stairway of perfection? So I looked in the Bible for some hint about the lift I wanted, and I came across the passage where Eternal Wisdom says: 'Is anyone simple as a little child? Then let him come to me.' To that Wisdom I went; it seemed as if I was on the right track; what did God undertake to do for the child-like soul that responded to his invitation? I read on, and this is what I found: 'I will console you like a mother caressing her son; you shall be like children carried at the breast, fondled on a mother's lap.' Never were words so touching: never was such music to rejoice the heart—I could, after all, be lifted up to heaven, in the arms of Jesus! And if that was to happen, there was no need for me to grow bigger; on the contrary, I must be as small as ever, smaller than ever" (*Autobiography of a Saint,* pp. 248–249).

Six weeks before her death she said to her sister, "Sanctity does not consist in these and those exercises and achievements. It consists in a disposition of the heart which allows us to remain small and humble in the arms of God, knowing our weakness and trusting to the point of rashness in his fatherly goodness. . . . It is sufficient to humble ourselves, to endure our own faults with meekness. That is true sanctity. If there were not often something offensive to God in our faults, we would have to commit them deliberately in order to remain humble" (quoted in *The Hidden Face,* p. 338).

These are startling statements when put alongside many of the traditional ideas about holiness. Thérèse's stress on the need for complete spiritual poverty and dependence on our Abba for everything makes her one of the outstanding practitioners and teachers of the abba prayer.

Her "little way" may seem easy. It is, in reality, one of the most difficult tasks of the spiritual life. She has been sentimentalized and her doctrine distorted too often, and she should have been called not "the little flower" but "the little rod of tempered steel." Humanity's flawed state means that we have a persistent desire to repudiate "the everlasting arms," to jump down and run off to a place *we* choose to do the things *we* feel like doing, in disregard of both our earthly and heavenly fathers' wishes, and in disobedience of their orders.

To choose to control and deny these wayward impulses, to stay where we are and be one of God's unnoticed and unsung instruments is possible only with the help of grace, the sternest self-discipline, and permanent, complete abandonment. Thérèse saw herself as one whose vocation it was to pass on to others whatever her Abba gave her for them. She was only the humble intermediary, the servant who is used, and whose accepted role is to obey. She was the little child who is naively—but in this case entirely justifiably—certain her "daddy" can do no wrong and so will never make a mistake. Therefore whatever he wants her to do, he is to be unquestioningly trusted and obeyed.

This is the abba prayer's quintessence. She became an adept at it in a very short time and as a consequence died a saint at the age of twenty-five.

Such abandonment is one of the sure signs of having attained transforming union.

So although we may not find the abba prayer quite the obvious "short cut" she did, we will certainly have to learn to practice it in one way or another, for it cannot help but be a source of basic peace and security to us. It will enable us to accept our inevitable humanness in humility, trusting God to make it the means of his grace to others and ourselves. It will simplify life and at the same time infuse into us an indefinable strength that will enable us to rise up on eagle's wings. We shall affirm from personal experience the truth of what the psalmist says:

> He who dwells in the shelter of the Most High
> and abides in the shade of the Almighty
> says to the Lord: "My refuge,
> my stronghold, my God in whom I trust!"
>
> It is he who will free you from the snare
> of the fowler who seeks to destroy you;
> he will conceal you with his pinions
> and under his wings you will find refuge. (Ps 90:1–4)

THE SURROGATE FATHER:
IN MEMORY OF L.T.B.

I had nowhere to go and you left your door open for me.
I had no one to turn to and you beckoned me.
I had nowhere to lay my head and you held it against your heart.
I was aching for comfort and you put your arms around me.
I was a waif and you gave me heart room.

I was hurting and you soothed me tenderly.
I was covered in wounds and you dressed them.
I had a gash in my side and you staunched the blood.
I had thorns in my flesh and you pulled them out.
I had been beaten up and you helped me to my feet again.

I was humiliated and you assured me I mattered.
I was rejected and despised and you affirmed me.
I was sneered at and you respected me.
I was slandered and you praised me to others.
I was treated as an outcast and you said I was a queen.

I had no friends and you befriended me.
I was forsaken and you stayed beside me.
I was without support and you were my rock.
I needed to confide in you and you understood.
I was afraid and you reassured me.
I was in darkness and you lit a lamp for me.
I needed a guide and you gave me your wisdom.
I was starved for love and your arms cradled me.

I longed for Christ and you brought him to me.

Joyful Slaves

Transforming union inevitably expresses itself through the prayer of total self-offering, which is also the succoring prayer of those who have become God's joyful slaves and hasten to serve him in others.

In biblical terms servant, bond-servant, and slave are synonymous. Isaiah speaks prophetically in chapters 40–55 of the Messiah as the suffering servant who, though innocent, dies to atone for the evil done by others. He is God's instrument of salvation. He is a sin offering, willingly conniving in his own suffering and sacrifice that others might be healed. His defeat is a victory, his death a blessing for others. Clearly he foreshadows Jesus, the Christ, the Savior, yet to come, and his destiny.

The New Testament takes up the theme in a number of places and applies it to Christ, with clear reference to his passion and death. Jesus testifies to its prophetic message about himself. In this way, the profoundest possible meaning is given not only to his, but by extension to our own, individual sufferings (and subsequent resurrection) and those of humanity as a whole.

When Jesus girded himself with a towel, took a basin and washed the feet of the disciples at the last supper, he deliberately did what was considered a slave's work, and told them to do likewise. He was living out his command that his followers were not to seek out positions of honor and importance, but rather those that were menial and despised, in order to be slaves of all. Yet on the same evening he also tells them they are no longer slaves but his friends and confidants. Obviously we can paradoxically be both at the same time! As Christianity is full of paradoxes, this should not surprise us. There are various levels of meaning, and we are meant to have the discernment to choose the one that applies.

In the third syndrome God is our Abba, and we enjoy the glorious liberty of his daughters and sons by adoption. Yet Jesus urges us to be as he was—not the obviously conquering Messiah, but one who "did not cling to his equality with God but emptied himself to assume the condition of a slave" (Phil 2:6-7). In doing this he "became as men are," for, theologically speaking, slavery is our natural state as beings dependent upon God for the gift of life itself and all that is an adjunct of it.

It is only by his special grace, and through the Son's identification with us, that we have also become children of the Father, and heirs with Christ.

In their letters, the apostles refer to themselves as "servants" (i.e. slaves). Paul, so proud of his Roman citizenship, yet writes, "So though I am not a slave of any man, I have made myself the slave of everyone, so as to win as many as I could" (1 Cor 9:19). In the process he "must go through the pain of giving birth to you all over again, until Christ is formed in you" (Gal 4:19).

Peter tells us that we "are slaves of no one but God" (1 Pet 2:16), yet, by extension, that makes us slaves of Jesus, God incarnate, and further still of all human beings with whom the Lord identifies himself in his extended incarnation.

Paul begins his letter to the Romans, "From Paul, a servant of Christ Jesus who has been called to be an apostle . . ." In 2 Corinthians 6, he writes, "We prove we are servants of God by great fortitude in times of suffering"—plus a whole array of other virtues faithfully practiced.

He makes his supreme statement of his own servanthood when he writes to the Colossians. After telling them that he has "become the servant of the good news" in order to preach it, he adds, "It makes me happy to suffer for you, as I am suffering now, and in my own body to do what I can to make up all that has still to be undergone by Christ for the sake of his body, the church. I became the servant of the church when God made me responsible for delivering God's message to you. . . . The mystery is Christ among you" (Col 1:24-25, 27). There are tremendous depths of theological meaning and implications in this commitment of Paul's.

He feels so "devoted and protective" toward the Thessalonians that he is "eager to hand over to [them] . . . [his] whole life" (1 Thess 2:8). He tells his beloved Timothy that his "life is already being poured away as a libation" (2 Tim 4:6).

Jesus urged us to go out and tell the good news to all the world. This means that we are to participate in an effective apostolate. Such an apostolate needs several key characteristics, or, rather, we as apostles need particular virtues which, of course, will inspire and shape our apostolate.

1. We must be called to it by the Spirit. This means that we do not choose it for ourselves, but it is chosen by God for us, irrespective of how we feel about it, or whether we think we are fitted for it, or whether it can be reconciled with our life pattern, or whether other workers in that field welcome us or groan at the mere thought of our joining them. Our "call" will not necessarily be precise and clearly indicated. We may simply be nudged toward it in a fog over a shorter or longer period, till it is the only course open to us.

2. We have no reservations in our gift of self to God, and, by extension, to those who share with him Christ's extended incarnation. This means that we will go anywhere, do anything, serve anyone the Spirit indicates.

3. We are persons of deep, persevering prayer, with a tried and tested faith that assures us this prayer is our lifeline to an effective apostolate.

4. We are not aiming at "results" that can be seen and verified. We know the Spirit works mostly in secret, and what we consider positive and desirable results are not necessarily so from the divine viewpoint. Yet we also have a rocklike faith that, as long as we are fully committed and abandoned, effective results, according to God's will, not ours, are certain to ensue. We may not know what they are until after we die, but this does not worry us.

5. Our motivation is love. This love cares about the well-being of others at all levels, but especially for their eternal welfare. Whether love is expressed through the corporal or spiritual works of mercy (which, anyway, are inseparable) is a matter of indifference to us. We do not make and choose our own vocation, but accept it from the Spirit as God's will for us.

6. We love God's will passionately and with complete dedication. In this we follow Jesus, considering ourselves slaves of God. "Nevertheless, not my will be done, but yours," is our constant implicit if not explicit prayer.

7. We burn with the need and desire to pass on to others the blessings of faith, hope and love we ourselves have received from our Abba. We are so full of gratitude for all the Lord has done for us that we can never do enough to repay him, and we are convinced, with Teresa, that "bringing him souls" is what Christ wants "most of all," for this was why he became incarnate, underwent his kenosis, and "assumed the condition of a slave."

8. Our attitude toward what we are doing and the people we help is one of joyful dedication and service. We feel that it is these others who are doing us a favor rather than that we ourselves are dispensing favors. In this we are doing our best to be true disciples of the divine Slave who, "for the sake of the joy which was still in the future, endured the cross" (Heb 12:2). It is our spirit's faith and hope that are our driving force rather than any emotional satisfaction on a comparatively shallow level. The joy we feel is ethereal because spiritual and infused by the Spirit. We "are sure of the end to which [our] faith looks forward, that is, the salvation of [our] souls" (1 Pet 8:9), and of the souls of all those we minister to.

9. Such characteristics of the joyful slave are formed in prayer, and sustained by and expressed through it and the graces for which it is a channel. We know that everything we now do as God's servants is prayer, and that is why, at the end of time, it will be revealed as abundantly fruitful for the kingdom. All things work together for the good of those who love the Lord, and for those they serve in that love. As partners with Christ in his redemptive work, we know we are truly succoring his body. We are content to work only for love, leaving the results to him.

When we reach this stage of dedication in servanthood, we offer God "an unending sacrifice of praise" (Heb 13:15) through all we do. Our spirit of tranquil, abandoned self-immolation in union with Jesus is enriched by the Spirit's gifts of "love, joy, peace, patience, kindness, goodness, trustfulness, gentleness and self-control" (Gal 5:22). These are expressed in self-giving to others, so that they

are enriched with us. They are drawn to Jesus and his message of
hope. They experience him directly through our ministrations, and
we wonder at the ineffable privilege of being used to give Christ
to our neighbor. This is made clearly evident if we are eucharistic
ministers to the sick and housebound. Because we know it is he who
is really doing the work while we are mere instruments, we are not
tempted to vainglory.

If we are in the state of transforming union when this great
privilege of being used as a slave is bestowed on us, we shall be
acutely aware that what is passing through us cannot help but be
a powerful force for good in the contemporary world. Salvation
includes liberty, justice and peace in terms of human and social
needs. It means the outlawing of tyranny, oppression, torture,
poverty and starvation. It frees from the gnawing dread that the
future will be blanked out by global warfare, nuclear nightmare, or
the final destruction of planet earth's resources and environment
and hence the death of the human race.

We care fervently about all these human concerns, and in one
way or another are involved in dealing with them. The risen Lord
wants to elevate all into the glorious liberty of the children of God,
and to bless and renew our planet, but we ourselves must labor to
bring it about. Through our very life-style, attitudes and actions, we,
as slaves of God, and of everyone, show our concern about the evils
that oppress people and despoil their living spaces, as well as threatening doom for the future.

The whole earth and all the peoples living on it interact. We are
one world and one people and one eco-system. We do what we can
to bear witness to our conviction that reverence and due care for all
life and our whole environment are what God requires of each one
of us. As good stewards to whom he has entrusted so much, we do
our best to give an example of unwavering trustworthiness.

We believe that in such ways we are channels for the infinite
healing powers of the Trinity, and that these are expressed through
us in both visible and invisible ways. It is our faith that, by willingly
embracing an inner state of slavery (which is really the same as full
abandonment to divine providence), we are being used indiscriminately as a means of pouring out for the whole world the graces God
wills to give us for the human race's ennoblement.

We believe. We hope. We love. And we go on working, expecting little rest in this life, as does any devoted slave.

Jesus said, "Go out and proclaim the good news to all the world." The good news is that he has risen indeed, and we are raised up in and with him. We are free. The liberation from sin and slavery of the whole human race is implicit in his resurrection. Our work is to make it explicit. There are innumerable ways of doing this, just as there are innumerable apostolic works that need doing. The Spirit has endowed each of us with natural and supernatural gifts that we are to use to glorify God in the third syndrome.

During the long years of purification, we have already been at work in various ways and places, helping and healing as best we could and struggling with ourselves and our own needs at the same time. Our labors may or may not have borne obvious fruit. The hidden seeds we have sown through them, that are perhaps still growing in darkness and obscurity, are every bit as important as any fruit we can see and measure. Their advantage is that we cannot pride ourselves on what is hidden and unknown both to us and to others, and so we are helped toward a deeper humility.

Being raised up in the Lord and transformed by union with him places us on a new level of being, in a different dimension, where grace and the Spirit predominate in our lives, within and without. We are now immeasurably more effectual in apostolic work and servanthood because we are so open to the risen Lord's influence, so abandoned to his usage, so flexible to any change of direction he requires, so free of self-seeking and the need to manipulate, so at peace with him, ourselves and others, so unobstructed in conveying his grace and love to others.

Wanting only his will in the way and at the time and place he chooses to express it means that he can select and mold our apostolate for us. This may entail a continuation, on a more selfless level, of what we have already been doing. It may mean a dramatic switch to something quite unexpected, and demanding in a way that calls for our heroic abandonment because we feel, and are, painfully inadequate.

Lay women and men in our times have been inspired to start new movements that have spread across continents and in various ways brought the new life of the risen Lord to innumerable people.

God gave them the energy and enlightenment to perform a special work, and the Spirit led them through their own docility and love of God and neighbor.

For each of us in the third syndrome there is a personal task that God has chosen for us. Our initial responsibility is to open ourselves, shedding all pre-conceived notions, to find out or be shown what it is. Then in a spirit of joyful servanthood, we move forward to embrace and live out this God-given vocation in faith that, with his help and guidance, it can and will certainly be productive both in time and in eternity.

CHESS

You can do what you like. You know that.
I don't have to keep on telling you.
Yet I do.
Maybe it's to reassure my occasionally quailing self
that even while you're doing exactly as you like
irrespective of my desires or plaintive outcry
I can't come to any real harm.

Harm, that is, as you see it.
There are times when you and I
differ about what is harm and what is not.
You always win, of course.
Winner, take all. (You do.)
My main role is keeping my hands wide open,
upturned, relaxed,
here, resting on my knees.
You do the rest.

My life becomes a chess game that you play,
you, the chess-master, world champion,
universal victor over all systems,
opponents, dissidents and wreckers.

I've got to hand it to you—
you do know how to play.

I am merely the board you play upon—
your will one set of pieces,
the circumstances of my life the other.

Consoling Aridity

There are two kinds of aridity—crucifying and consoling. The first belongs to the time when, consciously or unconsciously, we are fighting God. The second comes when there is peace in the depths and these are saying to him, "Yes—whatever you do with me, it's OK by me." There is now no struggle to produce this full consent. It comes spontaneously and continuously.

Crucifying aridity is part of the birth struggle to emerge into the prayer of pure faith. It is like gasping for air—needing an oxygen mask and not having one. It is the stifling experience of God's absence while faith stupidly and stubbornly goes on affirming, "You are there, nonetheless, in the ancient place" (Ps 22).

It is the loneliness of the long-distance runner who runs in the dark with some strange kind of night-sight to help him "see" a way that is not a way, and avoid obstacles that seem real yet dissolve away before him in the fog. He knows he has a destination, but cannot visualize it. He gasps in the extremity of his effort, longing for water, for a compress on his forehead, for the chance to float without any striving at all in some everlasting stream of solace.

Crucifying aridity belongs to the depths of the night of faith where we have such a fierce thirst for a God who never comes that we feel we are being dismembered in our helpless longing. Only our battered faith keeps us shakily in one piece.

The grace of being transformed in resurrection love-life dramatically changes the nature of our aridity. It ceases to be that of Jesus on the cross crying out, "I thirst!" and becomes that of the well-equipped traveler in some strangely beautiful desert.

We felt before as if the aridity was slowly killing us. Now we consolingly experience this desert as one of the loveliest places we have ever been to. We are entranced by its vast perspectives, clear sunlight, fascinating land forms, its sparse, unfamiliar flora and fauna that burst into exotic flowers and new growth whenever the rare showers sweep across the dunes. All these encourage us to continue our journey. We are aware of life and beauty where before we could register only death and bleakness in a lunar landscape.

Whether we travel mostly in desert aridity, or in what Teresa frequently refers to as "favors," is irrelevant in resurrection love-life. We are graced in our depths, and the surface conditions are only the accidents, not the substance. The Spirit has given us insight into how purifying aridity is in its work of fostering selfless motivation. To continue to love and serve God while lacking any emotional balm, to go on praising and thanking his unadorned will—these are signs that we indeed love him for himself, irrespective of the manner in which he chooses to make his visitations.

Aridity that persists is both humbling and boringly uneventful, yet at this stage we are grateful to be humbled, and the uneventfulness is so tranquil that we could not feel we were being crucified by it as in the earlier stages of our journey. Consequently, we are never tempted to abandon prayer, no matter how emotionally unrewarding it may be. Somehow we are reassured that, in spite of persistent distractions in the upper levels, where the intellect and memory operate, and our lack of affectivity, prayer *is* happening in us, in the manner and form that matter.

In this desert we praise God just for being God. We trust him so fully that we experience no ache for the assurance of feeling in the emotions either our love for him or his for us. We know that our mutual love has been sealed for eternity. The reality of it is established in our depths. For as long as it is God's will to keep us on this starvation diet that is at the same time so mysteriously fulfilling, we remain content with it.

> They who trust in him will understand the truth,
> those who are faithful will live with him in love;
> for grace and mercy await those he has chosen (Wis 3:9).

We certainly trust in him at this stage, for experience has taught us that everything he does and lets happen is for our good, and though we cannot understand at the time, later we shall, even if we have to wait till the next life. We have indeed been faithful in following him all through the years of being "tested like gold in a furnace" and being "accepted as a holocaust" (Wis 3:6), and now there are no obstacles left to our "living with him in love." We have been "chosen." Recognizing these facts, we see that we have done our best to fulfill what was required of us, and now his "grace and mercy" are permanently ours. We are aware of this as a present reality in our life.

It is this sense of permanence and chosenness that remains firm in us whatever happens, so that aridity cannot distress and in fact consoles.

The prayer of consoling aridity is a peaceful state. It is also a purifying one. Every day that we endure it in quietly loving abandonment, we are being more thoroughly cleansed and so are entering further into transforming union. Therefore such aridity is a genuine grace and blessing. It comforts us even as it purifies, inviting us to advance further into the stillness of waiting in the doing-nothing prayer.

Because there are no disturbances in our relationship with God, whether of a positive or negative nature, and because there is such peaceful simplicity in this relationship, it brings the consolation of unfluctuating security. The busy intellect still causes distractions through memory, making plans, rerunning well-worn tapes, using the imagination idly in various ways, but we are aware that all this is only on the surface—as Teresa says, only the children playing and making a noise in another of the interior castle's rooms. The deeps remain calmly absorbed in God and the certainty that his purpose will reveal itself eventually. Resting in God in the Abba prayer, our will is merged entirely with his. Our awareness of the actuality of such close union comes through infused faith that it is so.

The prayer of consoling aridity consists in abiding serenely in this emotionless awareness of presence-union without the need of any other kind of reassurance or visitation. If these are granted, of course we rejoice. They are anointings that facilitate union, but are in no way necessary to it. Having "God alone" means just that. His indwelling needs no trimmings, though they do embellish it when and if they are granted.

Some saints such as Thérèse and Jane Frances de Chantal existed in pure faith almost ceaselessly, and found out how to be at peace and fulfilled in what they came to experience as consoling aridity. Others like Teresa seem to have been immersed in "favors" very frequently, though in the summit state of the seventh mansion even she writes of "turmoils" resulting from "some chance happening." She assures us that they result in no harm, but instead are of benefit since they provoke "great determination [not on any] account to turn aside from [the Lord's] service and from [the soul's] own good resolutions. On the contrary, these resolutions seem to increase, and so the soul will not make the slightest move which may deflect it from its resolve" (*Interior Castle* VII, iv). It is humbled but also strengthened by such trials, which include persistent aridity.

Lack of solitude and silence, coupled with necessary preoccupation with whatever duties and apostolate God has given us, can provoke the prayer of aridity. Teresa, no doubt taking herself as example, stresses that in the seventh mansion we are likely to get "less and less of outward repose" and all we can expect to enjoy is repose "of an interior kind." At this stage, God is demanding that we work concentratedly for the kingdom. Having granted us full union so that we have peace in the depths, he requires us to be indifferent to the surface distractions and even "turmoils."

Teresa reminds us that, anyway, "we should desire and engage in prayer not for our enjoyment, but for the sake of acquiring the strength which fits us for service." There is no more powerful prayer than a continuous act of perfect abandonment to our Abba made in a state of complete aridity, for it is the summit of faith. It also indicates perfect trust, renunciation, self-gift, obedience and praise. God is for and in us. We are for and in God. The ego is at last quelled and reduced to docile simplicity. We now know and practice pure love in and through the Spirit given us by Father and Son.

In the midst of peacefully accepted and loved aridity, we have developed the taste for the purely spiritual. Spirit meets Spirit in our depths in an ethereal manner that leaves the ordinary emotions bereft yet provides the profoundest of satisfactions. It is difficult either to pinpoint or to describe such delicate, almost imperceptible unctions. They become part of an arid prayer in which we renounce all consolations on more sensible and manifest levels, in favor of being deeply sunk in God in naked faith.

Such prayer occurs at "the bottom of the heart, and in the supreme intelligence, or, as the mystics put it, in the center of the soul, at the point of the spirit; it is a peace of unshakable rest, I will not say amid human revolutions, to which one is now hardly sensitive, but in the midst of all interior vicissitudes. For it is founded on unreserved surrender to the supreme will of God, with perfect confidence in his all-powerful goodness" (J.P. de Caussade, *On Prayer*).

Paul said, "This is the will of God—your sanctification" (1 Thess 4:3). The prayer of consoling aridity is all the while cleansing and sanctifying us. It ensures that at last we can work for Christ and serve our neighbor in purity of heart. All our earlier efforts bore only marred, though useful and sincere, fruit. Now comes the time for the bumper crop of perfect fruits of all kinds, blessed by God, and given for his honor and glory, not ours. Now we serve the kingdom as joyous slaves, the desire for any rewards has vanished and in its place is the grace of a will fully integrated into the divine will.

ARIDITY

In these dried up water courses
rivers can and did rampage.
They burst their banks to inundate
parched hinterlands, form lakes
in hollows, lap at hillocks' slopes,
flow and eddy, whirl and toss,
and then, receding, leave behind
the careless debris of abundant life.

But now the greening they induced
has withered. Caked mud has dried
and in the cracks the crickets shrill
their thin monotonous chant.
The sun is merciless. And in the nights

a moaning wind warns of deserts
waiting to take over.

                    I contemplate
the arid spaces and sit down and wait.

CLOUD OF UNKNOWING

This came by night. I woke
to gray, dense moisture clinging, motionless,
black macrocapa trunks becalmed
like Loch Ness monsters, rearing from mist
to plunge up into cloud, but frozen in the act.

My little house floats in the sky—
a space ship, visibility nil;
beyond the trees gray emptiness,
palpable nothing, silent, still.

I know the hills, steep as ski slopes,
flow in a frozen cascade to the beach.
I know the sea itself moves down there
in rhythmic, recurrent patterns, moon-beguiled.
I know. I believe. I hold fast to the truth.
But as for seeing and verification . . .
well . . . there's no proof.

                    I am
enshrouded in the cloud of unknowing—
a moist, static, gray obscurity, concealing all certainties.

Almost against the kitchen window every needle
of the macrocapa fronds glistens with a diamond—
droplets of light whose myriads no cloud can quench.

The Widow's Mite Prayer

The little story (Lk 21:1-4) about the poverty-stricken widow has deep spiritual implications. Her minute offering, despised by the rich and secure, was in fact of great value, for she "put in all she had to live on." Poor already, she made herself finally destitute by giving her last reserves.

Now her only resource was God.

If we contemplate the inner meaning of the parable, we find that the pharisaical people who consider themselves spiritually rich because they fulfill all their religious obligations, and pride themselves on doing so, are in fact the genuinely poor. This is because they withhold their hearts, their true selves, from God. Busy counting up all they give him and the resultant rewards due to them, they are deaf to his call, "Give me your heart—for this is all I really want. If you do that, the rest will follow."

The pharisaical are self-important, proud of their status and wealth (both material and spiritual), counting up their indulgences (which, thank God, seem to have been quietly disregarded by the official church since Vatican II), sure of a place of honor at the heavenly banquet table, despising the (apparently) destitute at the temple gate. Jesus had already condemned such people before he even saw the widow.

"Beware of the scribes who like to walk about in long robes and love to be greeted obsequiously in the market squares, to take the front seats in the synagogues, and the places of honor at banquets, who swallow the property of widows, while making a show of lengthy prayers. The more severe will be the sentence they receive" (Lk 20: 45–47).

Such so-called "religious" people are materialists, living on the surface of spirituality, deaf to Jesus calling them to attend to the one thing necessary. Unctuously pleased with themselves, blind to their pride, vainglory, ostentation and hypocrisy, they regard themselves as worthy examples to others of the righteous life, with the privilege of despising those they consider religious pariahs.

The destitute widow is in impressive contrast.

Jesus, who has eyes to see, and so reads the heart, knows what is in hers. Its hidden treasure of humility is what matters to him, not her lack of outward show. He watches her give away her last shred of self-ownership and reliance on the material, and knows that, by doing so, she has placed herself unequivocally in God's care, trusting in his merciful love and unending bounty.

"Blessed are the poor in spirit, for theirs is the kingdom of heaven" (Mt 5:3). Being poor spiritually in her humility, she has access to all the riches and resources of the heavenly kingdom. She does not need to worry about the next day now that she has freely given away all she possesses, for she trusts her heavenly Father, her Abba, to fulfill her future needs according to his plan for her. If she had not had this trust, she could not have had the generosity to give away everything.

Once we participate in Jesus' resurrection love-life, the widow's mite prayer becomes one of the deepest dispositions of our heart. Having been through the despoliation process of the passive purifications, we now know experientially that we are destitute, and so must rely on God's mercy and grace. We were starved for the holiness and beauty of the kingdom of heaven within, knew we lacked it, and relinquished self-love and self-will in order to receive it. Now that we are absorbed into it, we are only too well aware that the Spirit alone can nourish us and be our guide, inspiration and power.

Earlier, we tried to enter the kingdom by our own will and methods, only to find that we got lost in the desert with the wandering Israelites, the promised land somehow never eventuating through the barren, vitiating years that yet were branded with God's presence in fire and cloud.

The journey of despoliation taught us what spiritual poverty was—total reliance on God, total abandonment to his Spirit, total commitment to Jesus as the only way, truth and life. We learned to practice the prayer of pure intention and humble dependence. "Show me, Lord, your ways, teach me your paths. Set me in the way of your truth, and teach me, for you are the God who saves me" (Ps 25:4-5).

God wanted not less than everything from us, and at last we gave it at ever deeper levels as grace revealed to us hidden "riches" to which we were still clinging. Finally, we were led into that state of spiritual destitution that Thérèse knew so well, practiced and taught. The widow's mite prayer is one of peaceful simplicity. This means that we are content to be our unadorned selves before both God and humans. The time of striking postures and trying to impress is over. The time of spontaneous sincerity and guilelessness has come.

The Spirit knows us through and through and did so "from our mother's womb" where it created and shaped us to fulfill a destined task. Now all we want is to be shown that task and what we are to do to bring about its fulfillment as God wills it. Our passive openness to the Spirit arises from this certainty of being known, understood and led by loving Wisdom itself. How can we now fail to trust? The intention behind all our acts is simple and pure. Shorn of the riches of self-seeking and self-aggrandizement, we join with the destitute widow in leaving the results of those acts to God, for we intend to serve him obediently for his honor and glory, not our own, in however veiled a manner.

This is true freedom. The widow had no material possessions left. We have now no spiritual possessions of self-ownership and pride in our virtues. We no longer try to shape our lives to gain any kind of riches—on the material level, wealth, position, power, success—or, on the spiritual, holiness (according to our version of it), a place of honor at the Lord's table (we have had it proved to us that we deserve only the lowest place of all), adulation (from which we recoil, for we know how destitute we are before God, and that whatever we do or accomplish for the kingdom is done through the grace he gives so that we ourselves remain "unprofitable servants").

The widow's mite prayer often expresses itself as a peaceful dumbness and silence before God.

In a way, we now have nothing to say to him. Or, rather, it is all said by the resurrection love-life in our hearts that no longer needs to question anything he does. "I am dumb, I speak no more, since you yourself have been at work" (Ps 39:9).

The work of his Spirit in us over the years has brought us out of suffering and turmoil into peace and fulfillment. His wisdom and love have been so amply and convincingly illustrated that our trust is now unconditional. We have no need to argue or lay our case before him. He knows, and has always known, everything about us, and has worked his marvels for us. He will go on doing so till we die, and he knows best. He has proved that.

The grace of holy indifference makes us gently "let go and let God," leaving the results to him. Before his manifested omniscience, we are humbled, and if we happen to locate a stray widow's mite or two in some coat pocket or corner of a drawer, we immediately pass that over into his care as well. He, the expert manager of our spiritual finances (which belong to him anyway), will invest it well, and we have no desire to know how or why or where. We understand now the wisdom of giving him all, and then leaving it to him to deal with it in his own way. We wait and accept, accept and wait.

The relinquishment of final responsibility for our lives (which, paradoxically, means we become in fact more responsible in carrying out our duties and loving our neighbor, only we do it without tension and anxiety) creates an inner stillness which is in itself a quiet bliss.

To own nothing, in the sense of no longer clinging to anyone or anything, to have withdrawn from all property deals, means we are free to sit in repose by the Pool of Tranquillity, our open hands resting on our knees or in our lap, receptive of whatever our Abba chooses to put into them as he says, "I want you to look after these for me, and with them I give you also the graces you need to be my good steward.''

To do as he wishes we may need only to immerse ourselves in the Pool of Tranquillity and drink deeply of its living waters, so that we are cleansed of some impediment to grace that we had not realized was there. After this we will be able to act rightly.

Or perhaps all we need to do is lean over the pool to gaze at our image in it and that of Jesus glimmering through it, and realize that in some respects the two do not yet perfectly coincide. Then we shall do or suffer whatever is required to remedy the lack of perfect transformation. This may well consist of a more complete act of abandonment, or relinquishment, or humility, after which we shall be freer to act in accordance with God's will.

And then we shall also be even more closely identified with the destitute widow and her prayer life.

The widow's mite prayer is also concerned with living at peace in the here and now, not lamenting over, or craving for, the past, nor reaching forward eagerly and covetously to the future and its imagined delights and fulfillments.

Resurrection love-life is already part of eternity. It is participation in the kingdom within, God come to dwell in his creature, the aperture of consciousness wide open and the glory of the Lord flowing through it. And yet it is also firmly fastened in this world of time and place for as long as we are still in the body. It is in the here and now.

Sometimes an awareness that this is so almost results in a schizophrenic split. We seem to exist one foot in heaven, as it were, while the other is stuck in the earth's fertile mud, the kind the Nile leaves behind it after flooding—and we are required to do something explicit about it.

The widow's mite prayer and the inner stillness it bestows does not eradicate action from our lives, but it does curtail or economize it. This is so because our activity in relation to the duties and necessities of daily life is now purposefully God-orientated and God-directed, instead of being an uncoordinated frenzy of searchings for self-satisfaction, self-identity and worldly goods and success.

The clearest directive we have for conduct in the here and now, other than to love and serve God, is to do the same for our neighbor. In all the vast variety of possible ways of fulfilling this command there are certain ones that are appropriate, and others that are not. Our state of inner poverty leaves us wide open to the Spirit's guidance. We ask, listen for, and eagerly respond to its promptings, and then we act out of the love and wisdom supplied.

The whole purpose of resurrection love-life is to pour it out into a stricken world starved and agonizing for it—mostly unconsciously. It is the Spirit that guides us into either the corporal or the spiritual works of mercy, the active, contemplative or combined way of life, the married or single state, the neighbor next door or the one in a far-away land. Sometimes what we are meant to do is just wait passively here where we are till God sends us the person for whom he wants us to be Jesus, or opens the way for us to go where he wants us to be.

The important thing is that, though we remain always ready to be guided to action, we are also prepared to wait for the Spirit's prompting or guidance. The widow's mite prayer enables us to act or to wait while it purifies our motivation even more. Over-eagerness and precipitate action can be a sign of either lack of trust and abandonment, or of hidden drives for the self-satisfaction of being an important, visibly successful and efficient member of "God's chosen" busily about his work—only we happen to have "chosen" it ourselves, and he may be wanting us somewhere else at this very moment.

Jesus told his chosen ones to wait and pray between his ascension and the gift of the Spirit at Pentecost. By that time they were all proficient in the widow's mite prayer of humility and spiritual poverty. They had also received many of the graces and fruits of resurrection love-life. These reached their fullness with the descent of the Spirit which finally made plain what specifically they were to do, how, where, and to whom. (Perhaps it is not fanciful to equate this empowerment with what happens in spiritual marriage or transforming union.)

Maybe the freedom given by the widow's mite prayer and its relationship to good works and apostolic action is summed up in Paul's, "So though I am not a slave of any person, I have made myself the slave of everyone so as to win as many as I could" (1 Cor 9:19).

CROWNS

When the crowns are allocated
will I be there?

I can see you tossing them up high—
a juggler with magnetic fingers
that cannot miss a catch or fumble one
of those so coveted mementos to the ground.

Will you flip them indiscriminately at us
rather like a children's lolly scramble?
Or will your marksman's aim, so accurate,
drop upon our unsuspecting heads
the apt and shocking truth?

Then those so certain of a diamond-studded ruby
huge as an ostrich egg and set in Inca gold
may find a circle made of battered tin upon their brow,
while that old alkie beggar there
whose downcast eyes
look only at your deft and sandaled feet
puts up his hands to touch aghast
a headpiece like a conquering hero's crown
all brilliant with a hundred precious stones
borne on a grumbling camel's back from Magi-land.

I wonder what you have in store for me?
I can't say that I really care. I think
I'll be too dazzled by the glory on your face
to bother ascertaining if my crown
is made of tin or gold.

CONSUMMATION

The beauty of it seduced me
when I was still a small child
asking, "Who made me?"

The beauty hypnotized me. It glowed
so translucently at the edges of my eye-span
I could not encompass it. If I held out my hand
it slipped in radiant streamers through the gaps
of my spread fingers. I tried to kiss it
but it had no form, so that my eager lips
touched air as iridescent as a rainbow
and as intangible. I wailed aloud
with helpless longing, stretched my avid arms,
pleaded and wept. I could not grasp it.

And yet it rooted in my depths. From there
it sent up tendrils twining all about my life
shaping my destiny till I believed
that it was made for me—the pearl
of priceless worth my hungry hands would hold,
my parched lips kiss in reverential love,
my arms embrace, my heart be pledged to finally.

It did not turn out that way at all. The beauty
like an ignus fatuus danced tantalizingly
and always just beyond my reach. I never could
quite touch it. Its promise proved elusive,
till at last, capitulating, I decided
it was not for me. I was unworthy of its loveliness.

And then it hovered right above my head
and, sliding gently down, it permeated me.

The Prayer
of Perfection

In Matthew's gospel Jesus gives us the beatitudes and other teachings that call us to the very high standard of virtue God requires of those who seek him. He concludes his instructions, "You must therefore be perfect just as your heavenly Father is perfect" (Mt 5:48).

Considered thoughtfully, this appears to be an impossible ideal calculated to induce a sense of defeat before we even begin our journey toward resurrection love-life. Anyone who is not a starry-eyed, impractical romantic knows from experience that human beings are born and die imperfect, and that in between they manage to produce in their own and others' lives, and in society, an uneasy amalgam of good and evil.

If we examine our personal motivations and acts we find a similar dubious adulteration, while we recall the occasions when impotence before our own weaknesses almost persuaded us to give up trying to love God and neighbor, let alone doing it "perfectly."

Although we do meet people who seem to be what we long to be, but cannot for all our efforts, and the rare one who could even be a saint, the end conclusion is unavoidable. To be perfect as God is perfect is an impossible task for mere humans. We have to acknowledge that our Lady was the only perfect human being born on this planet, and that was because she was "full of grace"—which is God's gift of his own life and love—from her conception. She was free of that inner fault line that all the rest of us have, that danger zone of instability where cave-ins, earthquakes, eruptions, slips, and the rest can and do happen with possible catastrophic results.

In contrast to Mary, we are all born handicapped, some severely through adverse heredity and environment, some only slightly because of much more benign influences.

What is the remedy for potential despair?

We must balance up Jesus' seemingly impossible command with all the other things he said and did to prove his and our Abba's compassion and forgiveness toward all of us sinners and imperfect bumblers. Remembering the prodigal son, we need to run to the Father, even with the muck of the pigsty still on us. His arms stay wide open, and he is running toward us to embrace us, dirt and all.

We must remember and reaffirm the fact that Jesus proved his loyal backing of us by sending his Spirit as the channel for his own resurrection love-life to us, just as it was sent to Mary. We too are "overshadowed" with glory—muted though it must remain in this life. We too can become "full of grace" insofar as we cooperate with the Spirit's penetration and seeding by grace of Jesus within us.

Scripture affirms over and over again the Trinity's endless love and longing to help us succeed in the task Jesus set us. At every turn they lift us to our feet again when we fall, and give us strength to stumble on till at last we reach that summit of "perfection." As we come closer to it, we discover that it is rather different from what we imagined was required of us.

Many neuroses have flourished because of false expectations arising from misinterpretation of Jesus' injunction, and perfection*ism* is one of the worst.

Those afflicted by it have unreal, impossibly demanding ideals for themselves, and for others too. Inability to live up to them encourages scrupulosity, rationalizations, depression and even despair about themselves, and, toward others, intolerance, disillusionment, a judgmental attitude and difficult personal relationships.

They have set themselves a superhuman task, forgetting they have a constant superhuman helpmate who is ready to lift them up on eagles' wings of grace. Thérèse decided she would do little things perfectly and do them all for love, but she did not expect to be able to do this on her own. She envisaged a "lift" which would take her up to Jesus, since she felt incapable, in her "littleness" of climbing "the stairway of perfection." In the extremity of her clearly realized spiritual poverty, she gave her widow's mite of love to God, certain that if only she stayed small enough Jesus himself would carry her to heaven. She deliberately capitalized on spiritual childhood and fulfilled the beatitude of poverty of spirit so perfectly that she was canonized surprisingly soon after her death.

We have much to learn practically from her "little way." Anyone at all can follow it if they decide to do so. Her perfection was in her humility and trust. To her, being "perfect" as her Abba was meant opening herself widely and trustingly enough to enable him to pour his own riches of grace, love and goodness into her. It meant permitting him to give her himself to be her strength and holiness. Only heroic humility can be this receptive, yet she proved that her little way was for all "ordinary souls" and was even the fast lane to the perfection of love Jesus enjoined.

Our frail, flawed human nature cannot by itself love God as he deserves. Our only solution is to let him do our loving for us. This means sacrificing self-love and self-will, which is why the struggle is so hard, and why so many cannot or will not persevere in it or even set out on the journey.

In essence, Thérèse's little way is the same as Mary's fiat, as Caussade's self-abandonment to divine providence, as Francis de Sales' holy indifference, as Francis of Assisi's poverty, as John of the Cross' submission to the passive purgations, as Teresa's drive to attain that innermost center and sanctuary of the seventh mansion where she would finally merge with the indwelling Trinity.

Saints do not become so by "striving for perfection" as if they wanted to make money and hoard it in the bank as riches for the future. Holiness is in perfection of love, and love is proved not by hoarding and account-making, but by readiness to embrace God's will, *whatever that entails.* Since his declared will is that we love one another in the same way he loves us, this is an obvious invitation to perfect love. And if we are to love perfectly, we can do so only if he gives us his own love to use as our own. John of the Cross writes, "But in this awakening which the Spouse effects in this perfect soul, everything that happens and is done is perfect; for it is he that is its sole cause" (*Living Flame* IV, 16).

Perfection also consists in clinging to God and refusing to let go of him while we affirm in faith that "underneath are the everlasting arms" that will never allow us to fall unless we willfully struggle out of them ourselves. Even then they will never fail to reach out to catch us and lift us up again.

Perfection means that we do our best in peace, humbly aware of what a poor best it is, while we live moment by moment feeding on grace, like a nursling at its mother's breast. "That you may be suckled, filled, from her consoling breast, that you may savor with delight her glorious breasts" (Is 66:11). We can enjoy this "delight" only if we become little enough in spirit to be the equivalent of a baby. This in no sense means to become a weakling in character. Those in whom spiritual poverty, spiritual childhood and self-abandonment are highly developed have a steely strength—so much so that they can and do often endure martyrdom, interior if not physical.

The handbooks on the virtues to be cultivated, the vices to be avoided, the various sins, the stages of the interior life, and the rest are useful maps to help in examination of conscience and suggest routes of self-discipline. If they induce anxiety, lack of fluidity, self-mutilating perfectionism, pharisaism, then it is a sign that we are mistaking the recipe for the soul's real food.

When we enter resurrection love-life, the Spirit shows us all this with limpid clarity. The command to be perfect is not meant to make us victims of scrupulosity and anxiety, but to liberate us so we can live like the flowers of the field and the birds of the air. It is to remind us that our Abba knows what we need and will surely give it to us when it is the right time if only we open our hearts and hold out our hands in loving trust.

It is to seek first the kingdom of heaven within, which means the indwelling Three in whom we find our peace and fulfillment. Once we concentrate on their presence and care, "tomorrow will take care of itself," our "whole body will be filled with light," the everlasting light of truth and love, and our "treasure" (or "perfection") will be within, in the eternal Presence that is perfect Love itself, where thieves, moths and rust cannot invade and destroy (cf. Mt 6).

Perfection is being like the Canaanite woman who, though she knows she is an outcast and unworthy, persists in making a nuisance of herself before Jesus, until he yields and gives her what she asks. He does this because she has such great faith, and no threats or insults from others, or apparent indifference or rebukes from him, can deter her. She *believes,* and will not give up. Perfection is in believing, no matter what, and persevering, no matter what.

It is in Peter's humble yet dauntless affirmation, "Lord, you *know* that I love you!" One of the most moving sentences in the gospels, this heartbroken insistence, after having acted as if the exact opposite were the truth, is an indication of what perfection consists in: continuing to love and give oneself to Jesus even in spite of our weakness, desertion, betrayal ("I tell you, I do not know the man!"), fear and spiritual and emotional bankruptcy. The response of Jesus is to place the infant church in this weakling's care—precisely because Peter now knows irrevocably that without his Lord he can do nothing, but with him everything is possible. He has become a nursling who will prove that the Lord's strength is sufficient for him when he is crucified, like his Master, for his beliefs—but upside down.

Peter was exceedingly human, and therefore we can relate easily to him. A prayerful meditation on his first letter gives us insight into how to live in order to be "perfect" in God's sight as the true sister and brother of his Son.

He writes, "Put your trust in nothing but the grace that will be given you. . . . Be holy in all you do, since it is the Holy One who has called you, and scripture says: Be holy, for I am holy" (1 Pet 1:13–15).

An injunction to be holy is the equivalent of one to be perfect. We are able to obey it only by trusting in God's promised grace.

As the one who denied his Master three times, and then had Jesus turn and look at him, reading his heart, as he was led away, only to be subsequently reinstated and given a special ministry of caring, Peter can say, "Once you were outside the mercy and now you have been given mercy" (1 Pet 2:10), certain that mercy is one of God's most precious gifts. To trust in it is to be well on the way to perfection. (It was supreme trust in God's mercy that enabled Thérèse to penetrate so deeply into the mystery of spiritual poverty and childhood.)

From the depths of his own humiliation and heartbreak that his betrayal of Jesus caused him, Peter was given insight into the suffering servant's vocation now that he himself had been called to be "the servant of the servants of God." Perfection is in giving oneself, out of love, and in union with Jesus, to serve other people.

"He was bearing our faults in his own body on the cross, so that we might die to our faults and live for holiness. Through his wounds you have been healed. You had gone astray like sheep but now you have come back to the shepherd and guardian of your souls" (1 Pet 2:24). Peter knew the perfection of acknowledging his debt to his wounded Savior, of experiencing himself as a redeemed sinner who let all the shameful past drop from his hands and heart, while he fastened his gaze and will upon Jesus who had forgiven him. In this way he could "live for holiness" and Jesus would help him do so. He never had the least doubt of it.

His certainty that sinners like himself have only to turn to Jesus to be saved is perfection.

"And if it is the will of God that you should suffer, it is better to suffer for doing right than for doing wrong" (1 Pet 3:17). There is a serenity in these words, an acceptance of the here and now, a laying gently aside of the past, a trusting willingness to face the unknown future without needing or desiring to probe and be anxious about it. In this is perfection.

Such a person "is not ruled by human passions, but only by the will of God" (1 Pet 4:2). Peter had seen his Master being ruled by that will and enduring his passion as part of it. And he had witnessed the resurrection and the Spirit's gift of its own love-life, as the fruit of the crucifying aspect of that will, bringing the Savior's sacrifice out of the darkness of apparent absurdity into the "glorious light" (1 Pet 2:9) of the risen Lord's indwelling presence. Peter knew whom and what and why he loved, he gave his whole heart to it, and in this was perfection.

He knew from experience that "love covers over many a sin," for Christ's love had cloaked him in tender forgiveness. As proof, he had been given a "special grace" of "feeding the flock" so that he could expiate his sin and his weakness by putting himself "at the service of others" knowing that, in doing so, he served his Lord, obeying his orders "so that in everything God may receive the glory and power forever and ever" (1 Pet 4:9–11).

To do everything for the honor and glory of God is perfection of motive. Whether we succeed or fail in our own or others' opinion is something for us to exercise detachment about, for only God knows the final results of each chain of events we initiate by that first act of love and homage.

To "share in the sufferings of Christ" is cause for gladness because it leads to participation in the glory of his resurrection love-life. "It is a blessing for you when they insult you for bearing the name of Christ, because it means that you have the Spirit of glory, the Spirit of God resting on you." We must simply "trust [ourselves] to the constancy of the creator and go on doing good" (1 Pet 4: 14–19).

To have the Spirit's glory is to have perfection by proxy, as it were, and be immersed in resurrection love-life. We cannot make this glory for ourselves—it is a free gift of grace to enable us to work and suffer for the kingdom. Our work is, in humble trust, to "go on doing good" in whatever ways are open to us in our daily lives and the ministry God has assigned to us. This is perfection, as long as we are doing, with the help of grace, the best we can.

We can comfort and inspire one another with Peter's example and words, "You will have to suffer only for a little while" (compared with an eternity of bliss and love). "The God of all grace who called you to eternal glory in Christ will see that all is well again. He will confirm, strengthen and support you. His power lasts forever and ever. Amen" (1 Pet 4:10–11).

To have such faith and trust, such resolution to persevere, such reliance on grace, is to be perfect as our heavenly Father is perfect, for it is to fulfill that human destiny for which we were created, just as he fulfills his godhead by being perfectly Three-in-One.

DIALOGUE

"You took your time!" he chided her so tenderly.

"There were barriers all along the route
and someone had tampered with the signposts . . ."

"But surely you knew the way by heart!
In dreams, if not in actuality. I thought
I'd shown you every bit of it,
taken you along it personally
almost to the end! How could you
have lost your way? Even though
some signposts had been vandalized."

"You'll make me cry!"

                     His gentle fingers
stroked her cheek. "You couldn't—
even if you tried. No one ever mourns
or weeps once they've arrived and known
the true embrace, the everlasting kiss of peace."

"The barriers," she whispered, "they were real.
I tore my nails and made my hands all bloody
beating at them. And the muddling signs—
I got confused. I thought that I was going mad.
Storms and darkness. Voices jeering at me
glad that I was lost. And fog . . . I broke
my shoes. My feet were cut and blistered.
I cried out to you to help me—but
you didn't come. I tell you I was lost.
I called—you didn't answer. You—"

His fingers gently closed her lips.
"Hush now, my dear. My dearest love.
It's all past now. A nightmare. That was all.

A fearful one that blinded you
and made you deaf. And so you could not tell
I never left your side at all. Each moment
I was guiding you through night and storm and fog.
My arm supported you when all the signs
made nonsense. Those barriers you beat at
futilely I led you round by level paths
that wandered over flowery fields where larks sang.
I gave you rest there underneath some trees.
But you were blind and deaf and did not know . . .
And now you've reached your home. No more
nomad journeys. The search is ended. Can't you feel
the haven of my arms? My heart that beats
for you alone? My eyes that speak of love?
The nightmare's over. Sleep and rest.
Tomorrow we will celebrate together."

She rested then. And slept. At last she slept.

Soul-Friending in the Risen Christ

The tradition of soul-friendship in the church is ancient and respectable. Scripture reveals how in varying degrees it was established between Jesus and his disciples, and certain women, notably Mary of Bethany. It was a bond among the disciples themselves, and permeated personal relationships in the apostolic church.

Authentic accounts of profoundly spiritual and loving relationships between Christed people of the same or opposite sex exist in all periods up to the present. They are both moving and inspiring, though often misunderstood, especially when contemporary psychology that is divorced from spirituality ferrets into them.

Soul-friending begins hesitantly for many quite early in their life of committal to Christ, and for a long time will contain elements that need purifying. With her usual insight and common sense, Teresa writes about these earlier stages in Chapter IV, vii of *The Way of Perfection*. Imperfections are to be expected as we journey in faith through the desert of temptation, deprivation and trial symbolized by the wanderings of the Israelites on their way to the promised land. During this demanding journey loving friendships, though spiritually immature, can give valuable support and comfort.

They also occur between people who are not Christians, but these are outside the range of this chapter, which is principally concerned with soul-friends who, themselves having entered resurrection love-life, meet in the risen Lord, with all that that implies.

In such relationships, temptations against purity of heart and body are not present. Other, subtler problems of avoiding any element of I-It traps are also absent. We no longer need to use others for our own self-satisfaction, of whatever brand. It is not a matter of having to face up to and control such urges and manipulations. They have been dissolved away by grace in the deeper purgations as one of the prerequisites for entering into resurrection love-life.

Our loving now has its source in the Christ-love centered in us, and in our personal love-union with the risen Lord. He has become for us the most intimate of soul-friends that it is possible to have. Constant awareness, muted or heightened, of the living bond between us makes it impossible for us to debase any human relationship into one of user and used, for that would be to insult Jesus. Our whole concept of usage derives from our free abandonment to God's use of us. We want to be used by him for others. We have no desire or need to use others for ourselves.

So a fundamental trait of soul-friendship is the absence of intent and attempt to use the other for our own ends.

This does not mean we avoid making our needs known to the other, or deny ourselves the mutual interchanges and confidences that are the channel of spiritual help and support. These are among the great joys and blessings of soul-friending. Sharing the deep secrets of the heart uninhibitedly and with serene trust is an essential part of such graced relationships. If there are reservations and lack of trust on either side, there is not yet the fullness of shared love. Perhaps we have been betrayed in earlier life by friends and family members, and so are cautious of fully giving either confidences or heart. Yet soul-friends encounter each other in the Spirit, who has, by one means or another, through a chain of circumstances, made it possible for them to be closely associated, and has then drawn them together. Consequently, the fundamental nature of their bonding is different from that of any earlier relationships, and mutual trust results.

Such "drawing" has a flavor all its own, a completely wholesome taste recognized only by those who receive this special grace from the Spirit, and act on it. Sometimes a strong sense of recognition also comes. It is as if we have known this person well in a former life, or been involved with her years earlier, but forgotten all about it until now. However, this experience of familiarity flows from neither of these, but from Christ in each person recognizing and moving out to Christ in the other. At its deepest levels it may become almost an exchange of individualities.

What draws these two together, then, is not interests or aptitudes they may have in common and enjoy sharing—though, if present, these are an enrichment. The fundamental iron-filings-to-magnet attraction occurs because each recognizes and responds to a certain spiritual dimension in the other—that of resurrection love-life. The sharing and sense of security arise from this spiritual likeness that is more significant for them than any of mind, body, emotions or interests. Hence the term "*soul*-friends."

Being "brothers and sisters in Christ" means actually meeting and merging in him, because he is alive, real and active within us. The sharing and trust in the apostolic communities arose directly from their vivid awareness of the risen Lord's actuality in themselves and the other baptized.

"The whole group of believers was united, heart and soul. . . . Everything they owned was held in common. . . . None of their members was ever in want, as all those who owned land or houses would sell them, and bring money from them to present it to the apostles. It was then distributed to any members who might be in need" (Acts 4:32–35).

This sharing of material goods was only the outward aspect of the intense inner sharing of the whole community in Christ. They were indeed one in him, as at the last supper he had prayed they would be. Paul reveals in his letters how they were not always capable of living at this spiritual peak. Factions, rivalries and severances occurred only too often—and still do, alas. Even Paul himself and Barnabas quarreled so seriously that they parted company and Paul chose Silas for his traveling and apostolic companion (see Acts 15:39–40).

But the early church's convictions and practice of being one-in-Christ remained alive. It has continued to evince itself powerfully in certain Christian communities and between certain individual members of them. These were, and are, more permeated by resurrection love-life than others and more graced by the Spirit who draws them into soul-friendships of compelling holiness and intensity.

There are many authentic records of such soul-friending among the saints of both sexes. There have been, and are, innumerable others that have never been recorded, yet have ennobled and graced the lives of certain women and men, lay and religious, all through the centuries and into our times. "How these Christians love one another!" was said of whole communities. Such love-bonding of the whole devolved from the love-bonding between individuals which cross-fertilized the whole group with resurrection love-life.

Soul-friends are united in the love of spiritual affinity. In essence this affinity is concentrated in both persons' total surrender and devotion to Jesus, personally and intimately experienced as present within, and loving through them. This shared affinity in Christ is what characterizes soul-friendship and makes it different from all other kinds of human friendship, no matter how noble and beautiful.

Soul-friends not only love and share in and through Jesus established in them, but they do so because of him. He commanded, "Love one another *as* I love you" (Jn 15:12). Soul-friends love each other because Jesus tells them to, and they are able to do it in the same manner as he does, because of his indwelling. They cannot help but be "other Christs" in their loving, because they are fully abandoned to him. Jesus always loves everyone, and when he meets no barrier in us he pours love freely through us for others because it is his will that we love as he does, and he longs to express his love here and now.

He draws us into the circumincession love cycle of the Trinity where, glorified, he does nothing but love forever and ever. Having entered his resurrection love-life we are inevitably caught up in this ineffable, divine floating in endless love. The ways in which the Lord uses us will vary in relation to our individuality and our personal vocation. Love is dispensed through us so that no one we encounter is excluded from its orbit, yet intimate soul-friends will be few, partly because life circumstances may well prevent our encountering them, and partly because people living wholly in resurrection love-life are not too common in this life. The price required to enter into transforming union is far too high for most people to see any point in paying it. They would rather pay later on and "enjoy life" here and now. They find the spiritual dimension either a bore or incomprehensible.

Since the risen Lord retains his wounds, though glorified, soul-friends cannot expect that suffering will have no part in their communion. They remain human, with their own idiosyncratic faults and failings which yet are involuntary. On occasion hurt may be given unintentionally and received in lack of understanding, or grave misjudgments may arise. Inevitable geographical separations are likely to occur and obligations of vocation may prevent even corresponding regularly, let alone meeting. All they can then expect is the severe diet of no person-to-person encounters, and only that indefinable, deeply-rooted certainty that they remain united in the risen Jesus and therefore cannot be essentially separated.

Faith affirms the spiritual reality when no other kinds of affirmation are possible.

Loving in and through Jesus means giving love without either needing or wanting anything in return. It is a no-trading situation. Therefore grief at separation has a kind of purity not present in griefs soggy with self-pity and craving to possess. Our basic hunger to love and be loved is satisfied in Jesus, and so we can be at peace in human deprivation even though, paradoxically, we grieve.

Job said, "The Lord has given. The Lord has taken away. Blessed be the name of the Lord." Soul-friends concur fully with his act of abandonment. They do not feed emotionally on one another or make emotional demands. This does not mean that their relationships lack warmth, joy, tenderness, sorrow, and many other human feelings that enrich friendship. The holy tenderness between soul-friends and its exquisitely delicate modes of expression are part of the beauty of their communion in Christ. Jesus was and is human, and so are we. We express love through touch, embrace, caress, and with soul-friends such tenderness has in it no sensuality or even sensuousness, latent or overt. It is spiritualized, just as was Jesus' own physical expression of love during his incarnation. Perhaps if we think of the way love was expressed among the three members of the Holy Family we shall realize how the human body can be the vehicle for an exquisitely pure and holy tenderness.

The origins of such tenderness are deep within the Pool of Tranquillity. They have not the least taint of murkiness or desire.

Soul-friends possess inner freedom within themselves, and give each other a similar freedom. In their relationship jealousy and possessiveness have no part and their love is entirely without them. They do not impose their own ideas upon each other, or expect to mold a replica of themselves. Instead, each delights in the other's individuality as God delights in that of every person he has made. In becoming Christ we become more complete individuals and our personhood is fulfilled. Soul-friends rejoice in exploring each other's specialness, in constantly discovering new depths in each other and revealing them in themselves. Each is happy for the other to have additional soul-friends, knowing that this will enrich their own relationship. They can even say, "He must increase: I must decrease," if it becomes apparent their friend has found a deeper affinity with someone else in whom resurrection love-life is more fully developed.

Only in resurrection love-life can we safely say to ourselves and the other, "Love, and do what you will." This is so because it is Jesus doing both loving and willing through and in us, not we attempting to act as "free" agents. In effect, we are for the first time really free to love, because we are unhampered by drives and needs urging us to appropriate the other person to satisfy these. Able to choose at last, we are helped to do so wisely and well by means of the grace of discernment given by the Spirit.

Now we realize how many misconceptions were attached to our former ideas about love and loving. The concepts were distorted by our own involuntary cravings and self-seeking. When thwarted, we suffered, and even turned on the beloved. Now such fallacies have been dissolved away by the Way, the Truth and the Life coming to us in person. He has revealed to us the real nature of our aims and needs. His Spirit of Love itself enlightens us as to the nature and expression of eternal life and love. Jesus himself living and loving within us demonstrates it experientially. At last we know for sure what his love is really like, and all we want is for him to express it through us for others.

"Jesus, do my loving for me," we plead. He answers our prayer, and in the power and beauty of that reply we are at last able to love and do what we will.

This results in a marked increase of pure loving kindness in our attitude toward and treatment of other people in general. We are graced to see and find Christ in them, and to serve him lovingly right where he is. Since Jesus has become our first and most important soul-friend, he teaches us how best to love others and then leaves us free to do so. The possibility that we should choose or be attracted to anyone who could harm our friendship with him is now nil. In his Spirit we recognize those he himself has chosen for us to become intimate with. This is rather like arranged marriages, where the spouses perhaps do not meet till the wedding day, or at least not till after parents and others have solemnly weighed up all the factors and decided the couples will be suited and make a stable union.

Jesus and his Spirit have decided who our soul-friend partner is to be. They arrange circumstances so we meet, enlighten us so we are drawn to and recognize each other as spiritual affinities, and facilitate our togetherness so intimacy can be established, deepened and finally made indelible in eternal resurrection love-life.

This is one of Jesus' most precious wedding gifts to us in celebration of our spiritual marriage to him. It is the heavenly association of the blessed, localized in us here on earth, for the honor and glory of God, the spread of the kingdom, and the health and wholeness of his mystical body, the church.

HARMONY AND SILENCE SEQUENCE

I

The simplicity at the center
is where we both belong.
Here words have scattered
like birds alarmed
at the stone of silence cast among them.

This center is the place of miracles.
Home in upon it, claiming territory
there in the singing void. Listen
for the harmonies in silence, enter
the quietude of emptiness, be aware
of Who dwells here, exuding presence
penetrating as scent of lavender after rain.

II

We are both rather silent,
we two,
not saying much to each other,
I and you.

How then came about this
understanding,
this deep, interwoven, supple
bonding?

It must be that They took pity on
our dumbness
and gave us of their overflowing
vibrant oneness.

III

He saw that everything was good
and so the harmony began.
Kaleidescope of
colors, sounds,
mingling of waters
in cascading joy.

Rippling leaves,
tossing boughs,
foam swept back from waves,
birds darting together,
grasses undulating in the wind,
clouds merging.

Our eyes meeting,
our hands joined,
our laughter together,
our simple sharing of a drink,
our silences when close,

our hands passing bread and wine,
our penetration by His life and love,
our voiceless murmuring of heart to heart,
our spirits permeated by the Three.

All these He blesses and pronounces good.
All of them chant alleluias
combining with the universal harmony,
the diapason of the Trinity.

IV

Now that he is overshadowing us
and we begin to be caught up
in radiant rivers and streaming seas of light,
now we are flung upon the sun's corona,
ourselves become bright living flames of love.
Now, now the years race backward
till we are ravished by youth's vibrant vigor
while age's wise and disillusioned peace
grants us this calm acceptance of each other.
Now we are truly blessed (though scarred
and gashed as wrecks on rocks) become
these towering torches, lit and intermingled,
alleluia beacons.

V

You are precious to me
in the Lord.
God breathes you to me
when he speaks the Word.

May I be precious thus to you,
a treasure, God's gift,
received in reverence
from his heart's cleft.

VI

A dance in which the partners
though involved so intricately
do not merge.

A harmony in which the singers
though altogether separate
produce a heavenly duet.

A feast in which the two participants
eat nothing, yet entrance each other's palates
with delicate, unique delights.

A love in which the lovers
pledged each to a sacred Third
tryst only in his presence.

A unity in which those joined
remain absorbed in Someone else
revolving round His axis, not their own.

VII

He came into that womb
because he could no longer
contain his ardor for us.
It was bursting him apart—
a supernova of exploding love.

He had no option but to enter
the dark, pulsing enclosure
that was flesh, to submit
to its confinement, and with a human heart
learn what we suffer
when we try to give what only he can give.

Dimly groping, I half understand
some of what he must have felt

when my own heart expands
threatening to fragment my body's cage
with what can only be
him loving you through me.

And so both flames and wound—
insignia of the human heart he took
and let expand to break wide open—
find replicas in us, minute and flawed,
yet pleading to be used by him,
our all too human flesh
the victim of his love.

Children of Light

The juxtaposition of light and darkness occurs throughout scripture from the first chapter of Genesis to the last chapter of Revelation.

In the beginning God said, "Let there be light!" and there was light—an emanation from eternal, uncreated glory, streaming out to irradiate the whole of creation and be its shekinah. It permeates us, too, in our resurrection love-life, so that we reflect his glory and live in the fire of his holiness like the three young men walking about in the furnace and praising God.

Paul writes, "It is the same God who said, 'Let there be light shining out of darkness,' who has shone in our minds to radiate the light of the knowledge of God's glory, the glory on the face of Christ" (2 Cor 4:4-6).

According to Peter, God "called you out of darkness into his wonderful light" (1 Pet 2:9), and John tells us: "God is light; there is no darkness in him at all" (1 Jn 1:5).

Human beings tend to have a primitive aversion to darkness. Yet John of the Cross in his poem on the spiritual dark night of faith can write:

> O night that guided me,
>   O night more lovely than the dawn,
> O night that joined Beloved with lover,
>   Lover transformed in the Beloved!

There is one dark night in which we are lost and wandering forlornly in sin, and there is another in which we are graced, safeguarded children of God, being led by the Spirit through faith's night to the dawn of imperishable light and bliss.

One night is infiltrated by the evil influence of the Prince of Darkness, the other penetrated by the resurrection love-life of the Light of the World. In order to enter the second, we must renounce the first. Once deep in the second we experience ourselves as "sons of light and of the day. We do not belong to the night or to darkness" (1 Thess 4:5).

We have ceased to be partners with Satan in the "darkness" of sin, and though we are in the spiritual dark "night" we do not belong there, because God is calling us out of it to our final fulfillment in his light. Spiritual writers teach that we will not and cannot emerge fully from the dark night of faith in this life, that we have to wait till after death for the face-to-face beatific vision of Uncreated Light and glory. We are not equipped to bear its splendor in the bodies belonging to this earthbound life.

However, we do, here and now, experience a modified version of it, much as Moses must have done when God appeared to him on Sinai, yet shielded him with his hand from the impact of his unveiled glory. We cannot see God naked and live in our fleshly state. Resurrection bodies will be adapted to deal with such ineffable encounters.

We pray for our dead, "Let perpetual light shine upon them," yet a muted experience of that shining may be given us, as a special grace, in this life once the windows of our receiving apparatus have been cleaned of all the grime of sin and attraction to sin. Probably only those who have spent years in the deepest passive purgations of the night of faith will experience emergence into resurrection love-life as a dramatic change into light, and only those who have undergone entombment to a crushing degree will be released into the spaciousness of floating in endless love.

Such foretastes of blessedness, whether muted or intense, come after a lifetime of dedicated service to God and neighbor, during which motives have been purified and consolidated into the single one of disinterested love, and the will has become finally integrated into God's will. Graced into resurrection love-life, we then have an inner, intellectual, spiritual awareness of light in vivid contrast to the painful awareness of varying degrees of darkness during the passive purgations. There is a direct intuition of being pervaded by a gentle luminosity. We are experientially bathed in it. This special blessing and grace registers penetratingly as such, arousing reverence and awe.

At rare times the glow is also perceived with the bodily eyes in certain other people, and in nature. An awareness is given by the Spirit that all creation is permeated by everlasting light and kept in being by its rays. Without it, everything would cease to be, just as the earth and all on it would wither into frozen death if the sun stopped shining on us.

The experiential light reflects and shows forth God's glory. It is always there, but we become aware of it only when the Spirit charges our powers of perception with a special grace. Just as sunlight can shine unimpaired only through a window that is perfectly clean, so the light of glory can shine only in a soul that is without sin and filled with reverential love.

There are exceptions to this, as when, on the Damascus road, Paul was knocked off his horse, though he was still hating Christians, and instantaneously caught up into the spiritual glory of the risen Lord which, once he saw it, converted him. He changed direction and made a complete about-face literally and metaphorically. The experience must have been like a super-charged, electric shock—"shock treatment" in a spiritual sense, both light and enlightenment to the nth degree, and all in an instant.

Because the resurrection love-life state anticipates the heavenly one, an experience of light is one of its properties. There are records of a corona having been seen around holy people which even lit up their surroundings. It is an emanation of the glorified Christ within them. However, such extraordinary signs are not necessary adjuncts to resurrection love-life. The divine light usually remains hidden and purely spiritual.

In the Nicene Creed we refer to Christ as "Light from Light," and once he possesses us, he illuminates our whole lives with loving kindness, at the same time gracing us with a mysterious, compelling awareness of his transfigured presence. How could we possibly desecrate such glory? Reverence compels us to avoid all sin, to work and suffer to dispel it and its effects from the world, to seek, find and serve Jesus in our neighbor, and to cherish the whole of creation as a shining forth of his own divine being.

This reverence is one of the fruits of infused light, another manifestation of the indwelling's dynamic reality.

It is also part of the grace of awareness. In faith we believe in God-in-us, and his influence on our lives. The awareness of it as light is an adornment of the sparse faith reality, though it is not the reality itself. This remains within us, whether or not we consciously experience it as light.

On Tabor Jesus was transfigured so that "his face shone like the sun and his clothes became as white as the light" (Mt 17:2). Paintings of this event usually depict him as levitated, and Moses and Elijah likewise—that is, floating in endless love. The Father speaks to and blesses his Son, while he shows forth their mutual glory.

Horeb, Sinai, Tabor—they are all symbolic mountains (even if actual also) where God takes us apart to reveal himself and his glory to us. He throws his shekinah over us. It is like Elijah's cloak that he bequeathed to Elisha. Once we have it in our hands or round our shoulders, we can strike the waters of tribulation, and they will part to let us through.

Maybe dry-shod, maybe not!

All through both Testaments God's shekinah is seen, witnessed to and recorded for posterity: the burning bush; the pillar of fire in the desert; the shekinah hovering in the tabernacle and Solomon's temple—angels fill the heavens with glory to celebrate the birth of the Messiah; Jesus is transfigured on Tabor; he is taken up to heaven in a blaze of glory; Stephen, just before he dies, sees God in his heavenly glory, and his own face appears like an angel's to the sanhedrin; Paul is blinded when he looks upon the risen, glorified Lord; in his visionary account of the end-time, John witnesses again and again to the glory of God and of the blessed now signed finally with his name on their foreheads.

"It will never be night again and they will not need lamplight or sunlight, because the Lord God will be shining on them" (Rev 22:4–5).

And so the story of God's adventuresome relationship with the human race begins and ends with light, glory, shekinah. These are

signs of his presence and his love. They signal his ineffable otherness, and his desire to invade and possess us, his beloveds, his children of light, whom he has made in his own image, so his holiness
would emanate from us too.

The early fathers of the church had direct encounters with the
risen and ascended Lord's glory, absorbed it into themselves and
manifested it in their lives. This manifestation was usually interior,
invisible, infused, mystical and secret. The only outward sign, except in rare instances, was in the evident holiness of their lives.

Their personal, inner transfiguration showed forth through the
gifts and graces bestowed by the Spirit, and their outward effects of
prayer, humility, devotion, reverence, mortification, brotherly love
and attraction to a life of solitude, silence and extreme simplicity.
They witnessed verbally and by their manner of life to the indwelling and to what they called "Taboric light" experienced in the soul,
and at times through a holy monk's person as a visible emanation
from the risen Lord. They lived moment by moment the resurrection love-life, the extended incarnation, the continuous passion,
the third syndrome, the interpenetration with the Trinity, and from
this inner intensity of pure being-in-God grace streamed out for
the world.

There were some fanatics and deviates among them, and a
great number of both canonized and uncanonized saints.

Their spirituality, mysticism and consummation in love has
come down to us, often in a modified form, through the example
and teachings of countless holy women and men, canonized or not,
through the centuries to our own day. It is localized where it has
always been, in those hearts which Jesus has taken possession of and
is now using to convey his resurrection love-life to a sin-marred,
problem-tormented, threatened-with-final-disaster world.

"The light shed by the good news of the glory of Christ, who is
the image of God" (2 Cor 4:4), affirms through the centuries that
"the night is almost over, it will be daylight soon." It urges us, "Let
us give up all the things we prefer to do under cover of the dark; let
us arm ourselves and appear in the light" (Rom 13:12).

And so we persevere in faith, hope and love even when it seems
that the Prince of Darkness, not the Light of the World, has all the
power, and evil predominates everywhere. In our century, our glob-

al disasters multiply and are aggravated till the well-meant efforts of countless caring people appear to be nullified by the stupidity, greed, corruptness and violence of countless others.

The temptation to despair and quit is strong, but we are followers of One who persevered through torture and an agonizing death to emerge triumphant as the glorified, risen Lord of the Universe. He calls us to rise with him, reminding us that we can do all things in his strength when living as one with him.

Renewed, we get up and go on, with Paul's words to help us: "So stand your ground, with truth buckled round your waist, and integrity for a breastplate, wearing for shoes on your feet the eagerness to spread the gospel of peace, and always carrying the shield of faith so that you can use it to put out the burning arrows of the evil one. And then you must accept salvation from God to be your helmet and receive the word of God from the Spirit to use as a sword. Pray all the time, asking for what you need, praying in the Spirit on every possible occasion. . . . May God the Father and the Lord Jesus Christ grant peace, love and faith to all the brothers. May grace and eternal life be with all who love our Lord Jesus Christ" (Eph 6:14-18, 23-24).

THE SHELL FISH

There it was—clamped tight shut—
an enormous, gritty shell,
a primeval creature's slimy habitat.

Here, feeding on sea ooze, this organism probed
with boneless foot into dark crevices
slithered and crept on rocks and seabed debris,
then,
danger or intrusion threatening,
withdrew convulsively between
its two hinged doors it deemed impregnable
into its questionable haven. None
of its soft, vulnerable parts were left exposed
to be devoured, squashed or swallowed whole.

For decades you worked ingeniously
either to pry its refuge-prison open, or else
to touch its quailing pulp so reassuringly
the reflex to withdraw would not be activated.
You longed to stroke and love it, murmuring,
"Strange, fearful, deep-embedded creature, trust me."

But though at times it almost let you fondle it
dread overcame it. Its hard, protective doors
involuntarily snapped shut. It squirted
inky poison at you, slid into a narrow crevice,
became quite still, and rested, imagining you gone.

But nothing put you off or quenched your love.
You waited till the time was right, and then
meticulous and resolute, you plied your ancient tools
of grace and love to force the shell wide open.
Bending, you kissed its sliminess. It squirmed
within its violated prison and while
it thrashed about your blessing changed
its nature and its form, transfigured it,
dissolved away its shell and made all new.

A shimmering, agile, rainbow-colored fish,
graceful as a bird in flight, went darting
from your craftsman's fingers. It sped
to surface in the light, leapt in its ecstasy
right out into the air, and curving in its dance
immersed itself again and dived to nestle in your hands.

FLOWER POWER

Out from the crucified heart
the flowers keep springing. Their cycle
goes on so persistently that I am never
without those exquisite bouquets and posies
that brides carry or people toss
at ballerinas they wish to honor.

You turn everything into extravagant blossoms.
I marvel at your ingenuity and when
you laugh into my faded eyes and warn,
"Look out! Here comes another!" I hold up
my love-starved arms and find them festooned
with garlands—roses and carnations, iris, hyacinths.

Such heady scents intoxicate my brain
and subtle perfumes drift and tantalize
that with eyes closed I breathe them in quite drunk.
I feel your kiss upon the wounds, your touch
on every bruise and festering sore. You smile
and other flowers burst from every ancient scar.

The Amen Alleluia Prayer

❦

During the dark years of the deepest passive purgations it was the suffering Christ who indwelt us, sharing his passion with us. Once we emerge from entombment, it is the risen Lord who fills our life, his glory welling over into it as his sufferings did before.

"The glory of the Lord fills the whole earth," and some of it permeates us, and from that permeation streams out again for others in praise and adoration of the Trinity. "All of us, then, reflect the glory of the Lord with uncovered faces; and that same glory, who is the Spirit, transforms us into his likeness in an ever greater degree of glory" (2 Cor 3:18 — Good News Bible). There is in us a heightened awareness of sun-drenched, open spaces, instead of the dark, stifling enclosure of the tomb. Like a lark, the heart soars into that infinity of light, to praise the Creator and exult in his glory. Vaughan Williams' *Lark Ascending* expresses something of this artless, ecstatic flowing up into God of alleluias.

We are now branded with God's name on our foreheads signifying his affirmation, "This one is mine." This is his response to our own final commitment, "You are my God forever and ever, and I belong to you." With the apocalyptic angels we sing in our hearts continually, "How great and wonderful are all your works, Lord God Almighty; just and true are all your ways" (Rev 15:3).

The Babylon of our self-will and self-love has fallen before the assault of the Spirit's grace upon our innermost citadel where we still piped, "Myself for me!" All our walls have been razed, and in place of the pagan altar where we worshiped our own autonomy is the Lamb himself, resplendent in the holiness of his sacrificial love poured out for all of us.

The somber forces of self-destruction within us have been subdued and defeated. The Spirit's glory overshadows our whole selves and lives and lifts us up to join in the great "Amen," the diapason of praise that the whole of a redeemed and glorified creation is thundering for God and the Lamb triumphant. We see the world with eyes that now seem to have a capacity to perceive the inner reality of all that is and to find there Christ, the Lord of Creation, through whom everything was made and who has redeemed and stamped it with his mark in its very essence. All of it is praising and glorifying God, and our own hearts are one with this mighty chorus.

"Alleluia! The reign of the Lord our God Almighty has begun. Let us be glad and joyful, and give praise to God, because this is the time for the marriage of the Lamb. His bride is ready, and she has been able to dress herself in dazzling white linen, because her linen is made of the good deeds of the saints. . . . Happy are those who are invited to the wedding feast of the Lamb" (Rev 19:6-9). The church as a whole is holy because it is sanctified both by the sacrifice of Christ, the Lamb of God, and by the sacrifices of the baptized who have given their lives to him, and even been martyred in blood for their faith. We ourselves are members of Christ in his church, and he has sanctified us through the long years of our interior, hidden martyrdom as we struggled to open ourselves wholly to his love and his purpose for us. Now he has elevated us into the bridal state, claiming us fully and finally as his chosen ones. Now we feast with him in his resurrection love-life and know the true, lasting fulfillment found in him alone.

Because grace has gifted us with this love-life we are blended with the risen, glorified Lord, and already, although still on earth, we partake of his heavenly state of being. We have an acute—or more often muted, since we are still in the flesh—awareness of the divine Presence, a sense of being blessed beyond telling by his endless love and enfolded in his embrace. We are his brides, indissolubly one with him in his Spirit. We have a glorious wedding garment that he himself made for us with the help of our own puny efforts that attempted to express our total love and our longing to communicate it to him.

At last we are "ready," and he has acknowledged it by uniting himself with us "in the most interior place of all and in its greatest depths," as Teresa writes, (*Mansions,* VII, 1), and John of the Cross affirms, "[Here he] communicates to [us] the strength of love of his breast . . . in the inmost substance of the soul" (*Living Flame* IV, 13). Our response is a gratitude so deep and full that we cannot praise and glorify him enough, and so we keep longing to find new ways of doing so.

Because resurrection love-life is the life of the Trinity active in and through us, it knows no limitations. Providing we let it—and now at last we put no barriers in its way—it expresses itself just as it chooses right where we are and in the usual circumstances of our lives. The possible modes are countless, but usually it adapts itself to the particular gifts and potentialities of each of us as individuals, though sometimes it entirely disregards these and uses as an instrument someone who seems, in his own or others' estimation, to be in every way unsuited for the task.

However, each one of us is suited to the task of offering the prayer of praise and glory—on our lips, in our hearts, and through our lives, by loving in and through the Holy Spirit.

The Amen and Alleluia prayers are inseparable. In his poetic imagery depicting the heavenly state, the apostle John envisages the holy martyrs in their state of bliss, their robes washed white in the blood of the Lamb through their immolation, now standing in front of God's throne—that is, at last within the face-to-face encounter. They and the angels "worshiped God with these words, 'Amen. Praise and glory and wisdom and thanksgiving and honor and power and strength to our God forever and ever. Amen' " (Rev 7:12). Handel, at the close of his oratorio *Messiah,* catches some of the majesty and exultation of this chorus of praise and glorification.

Amen means "so be it"—we agree with everything, acknowledging its rightness, trusting in its eventualities, blessing its effects on us, affirming our faith in its final culmination when God will be All in all and "there will be no more death, and no more mourning and sadness, for the world of the past [will be] gone" (Rev 21:4).

In the resurrection love-life state, we are so graced that we are able to say Amen spontaneously to almost anything God lets happen to us, or the Spirit directs us to do or suffer. If there is a struggle before we can accept, it is brief and the conclusion is foregone. The struggle takes place not in our deep selves where our will is welded to God's, but in some of the irrelevant areas where involuntary fears (and perhaps our inner child) at times take temporary charge.

The deep, inward Amen never ceases its exultant chorus of assent, our joyous agreement with all that the Abba does and permits. "May it be as has been asked, said or promised," my dictionary gives as part of its definition for the word "Amen." Our Amen prayer means that we affirm our intention of never again getting in the way of our Abba's action in our lives, of always stepping aside and waiting patiently while he brings about his will. We are saying Amen before, during and after the conclusion of the process, and we know, as Dame Julian famously affirms, that "all shall be well, and all manner of thing shall be well."

This does not mean we never feel any perturbation. This is natural at times, but unconnected with a will in the Amen state. Our will knows and constantly affirms with Julian "that Love was our Lord's meaning . . . that ere God made us he loved us. . . . And in this love he hath done all his works; and in this love he hath made all things profitable to us; and in this love our life is everlasting. . . . And all this shall we see in God, without end. Which may Jesus grant us. Amen" (*Revelations of Divine Love,* chapter 86).

This ability to consent to God, to say "Yes, Lord. Certainly, Lord. Anything else, Lord?" to him, whatever he is doing, is part of resurrection love-life. The love in us is now Jesus' own love, and he always said and says yes to his Father. The life in us is the Spirit's own divine life, given to us that we might have life more abundantly, and the Spirit is the living expression of our Abba's living love for us. We are able to say Amen because we have entered the spiritual poverty of a true child of God, and, possessing nothing, we gladly accept as gift and blessing whatever our Abba offers us, and say, "Amen. So be it . . ."—or, colloquially, "It's OK by me. You do just as you wish. I'll go along with it." We remember that Jesus is not demanding "great deeds" of us, but only "gratitude and self-surrender," as Thérèse says.

However deeply we have been penetrated by Christ's resurrection love-life, always, until death, there will be opportunities to grow in it. This means trials and tests of abandonment, and having to struggle to give our full Amen assent as soon as they come. The struggle, like the athlete's training session, makes us work at deeper surrender, and our efforts make it easier to give assent when the next test comes.

God will go on requiring detachments. We still cling subtly and involuntarily to things, ideas, people, pet notions. We have been unaware of these adherences till now when the Spirit beams its torch into the shadowy corner where they lurk. Do we turn away quickly and pretend we have not seen? Or do we say, "Thank you for showing me, Lord. I deliver this possession—relationship, desire, ambition, fixation—trustfully into your care, and renounce it wholly from this moment. Amen"? The Spirit may show us we are cleverly and disguisedly exercising self-will over some small (or larger) matter. Do we tell ourselves, "Oh, that's not important enough to worry about. I mustn't fret over such trivialities"? Or do we say, "Thank you for revealing this to me, Lord. Amen to the pain this causes me, and to the effort of renunciation I now know I must make. With your help, I'll be able to do this. Amen. Amen"?

"Amen" and "Alleluia" are both potent as mantras. They are like two petals on the same flower. The alleluia shout of joy, praise, glorification and exultation is sung by the blessed in their face-to-face encounter with God. "A huge crowd in heaven [was] singing, 'Alleluia! Victory and glory and power to our God' " (Rev 19:1–2).

It is the cry of victory of those who have, in the Lord's strength, overcome the powers of darkness within themselves and in their lives. It is the upsurge of exultation in our hearts where the Christ, vanquisher of all darknesses, is now, as Light of the World, permanently dwelling. It is directed to the One who alone made the conquest possible by giving us his own power and resoluteness.

The Ode to Joy at the end of Beethoven's *Ninth Symphony* magnificently conveys the triumphant joy of the Alleluia-Amen prayer in uninhibited spate. Such immensely high floatings in endless love occur rarely for most of us, so we have to learn how to relate our Alleluia-Amen prayer to mundane matters, expressing it in a low key and with one cracked voice, as it were, since we are neither

Beethovens nor Teresa of Avilas. We need not worry about this, for all experts on the spiritual life and prayer affirm that our unitive love-life is best offered through the ordinary, unimpressive actions of our everyday life. These are transfigured—though we are seldom aware of it—because in the third syndrome we are at last enabled to live and act solely for the honor and glory of God. We seek not our own ends, but his, leaving the results to his divine providence, his Abba care.

This has become the general, established pattern in our lives. It may at times evince minor flaws, but consciousness of these will keep us "small and humble in the eyes of God." They do not mar our offering to him, since our intention is pure.

Though no one may hear our silent Alleluia, people do pick up its vibrations without realizing it, and sometimes it begins to change their own lives. They are invaded by the sense of something other than the material world—another way of being and seeing that has within it a compelling beauty drawing them into its sphere of influence, into an awareness of the numinous. The Amen-Alleluia prayer within us is the Spirit at work, and it commands us to carry on that work in our daily lives and with all whom we normally encounter.

When he gave instructions on how the Christian communities were to live out their faith and love, Paul was writing not for ecstatics in monastery cells, but for ordinary women and men like us, living and working and relating to one another through that work, their family life, their leisure and their worship. He told them, and, by extension, us, "Serve one another in works of love, since the whole of the law is summarized in a single command: Love your neighbor as yourself. . . . You should carry each other's troubles and fulfill the law of Christ. . . . While we have the chance, we must do good to all, and especially to our brothers in the faith" (Gal 15:13–14; 6:2, 10).

We live the Alleluia prayer when we serve others for Christ's sake; when we find and praise the good in them; when we are grateful, and show it, for their love and help toward us; when we are always on the alert to support and affirm them with acts and words of kindness and appreciation.

We live out our Amen when we humble ourselves before others' criticisms and negative behavior toward us; when we trust God in

the inevitable severances from those we love, through misunderstandings, practical circumstances, illness, accidents, death; when
all our plans for them and ourselves go wrong, and defeat on every
level seems our lot; when we "forgive each other as readily as God
forgave [us] in Christ" (Eph 4:32).

The whole Amen-Alleluia prayer is summed up and uttered
through loving, humble service to others with the motive of honor-
ing and glorifying God.

As Paul tells us: "You are God's chosen race, his saints. He loves
you, and you should be clothed in sincere compassion, in kindness
and humility, gentleness and patience. Bear with one another. Forgive each other as soon as a quarrel begins. The Lord has forgiven
you; now you must do the same. Over all these clothes, to keep
them together and complete them, put on love. And may the peace
of Christ reign in your hearts, because it is for this that you were
called together as parts of one body. Always be thankful. Let the
message of Christ, in all its richness, find a home with you. Teach
each other, and advise each other, in all wisdom. With gratitude in
your hearts sing psalms and hymns and inspired songs to God. And
never say or do anything except in the name of the Lord Jesus,
giving thanks to God the Father through him" (Col 3:11-17).

It is by such fruits that the authenticity of our resurrection love-
life is proved and we experience an indestructible love, joy and
fulfillment in the Spirit. Amen. Alleluia!

ONE

I am in God
and God is in me
as the pip in the apple,
the bird in the tree,

as the cloud in the blue sky,
the rain in the cloud,
the fish in its pool,
the seed in the clod.

As lovers united
in tranquil bliss,
as waterfall plunging
to canyon's abyss,

as lungs filled with fresh air
on mornings in spring,
as sunshine that melts the frost
all glittering,

as eagle in upper air
soaring and free,
so am I in my God
and God is in me.

We are together
by day and by night,
we gaze on each other
in delight;

a galaxy's splendor
is our marriage bed,
we merge there together,
love consummated.